# IMPORTANT

HERE IS YOUR REGISTRATION CODE TO ACCESS MCGRAW-HILL PREMIUM CONTENT AND MCGRAW-HILL ONLINE RESOURCES

For key premium online resources you need THIS CODE to gain access. Once the code is entered, you will be able to use the web resources for the length of your course.

Access is provided only if you have purchased a new book.

If the registration code is missing from this book, the registration screen on our website, and within your WebCT or Blackboard course will tell you how to obtain your new code. Your registration code can be used only once to establish access. It is not transferable.

## To gain access to these online resources

1. **USE** your web browser to go to: **www.mhhe.com/cushner3e**

2. **CLICK** on "First Time User"

3. **ENTER** the Registration Code printed on the tear-off bookmark on the right

4. After you have entered your registration code, click on "Register"

5. **FOLLOW** the instructions to setup your personal UserID and Password

6. **WRITE** your UserID and Password down for future reference. Keep it in a safe place.

If your course is using WebCT or Blackboard, you'll be able to use this code to access the McGraw-Hill content within your instructor's online course.

To gain access to the McGraw-Hill content in your instructor's WebCT or Blackboard course simply log into the course with the user ID and Password provided by your instructor. Enter the registration code exactly as it appears to the right when prompted by the system. You will only need to use this code the first time you click on McGraw-Hill content.

These instructions are specifically for student access. Instructors are not required to register via the above instructions.

Thank you, and welcome to your McGraw-Hill Online Resources.

ISBN 0-07-312607-1
T/A CUSHNER: HUMAN DIVERSITY IN ACTION, 3E

# Human Diversity in Action

## Developing Multicultural Competencies for the Classroom

*Kenneth Cushner*
*Kent State University*

**third edition**

McGraw Hill **Higher Education**

Boston   Burr Ridge, IL   Dubuque, IA   Madison, WI   New York
San Francisco   St. Louis   Bangkok   Bogotá   Caracas   Kuala Lumpur
Lisbon   London   Madrid   Mexico City   Milan   Montreal   New Delhi
Santiago   Seoul   Singapore   Sydney   Taipei   Toronto

## Higher Education

HUMAN DIVERSITY IN ACTION: DEVELOPING MULTICULTURAL
COMPETENCIES FOR THE CLASSROOM

Published by McGraw-Hill, a business unit of The McGraw-Hill Companies, Inc., 1221 Avenue of the
Americas, New York, NY, 10020.

Some ancillaries, including electronic and print components, may not be available to customers outside
the United States.

This book is printed on acid-free paper.

1 2 3 4 5 6 7 8 9 0 BKM/BKM 0 9 8 7 6 5

ISBN 0-07-301029-4

Editor in Chief: *Emily Barrosse*
Publisher: *Beth Mejia*
Senior Sponsoring Editor: *Allison McNamara*
Senior Development Editor: *Cara Harvey Labell*
Executive Marketing Manager: *Pamela S. Cooper*
Managing Editor: *Jean Dal Porto*
Project Manager: *Meghan Durko*
Art Director: *Jeanne Schreiber*
Associate Designer: *Marianna Kinigakis*
Cover Designer: *Jenny El-Shamy*
Cover Credit: *©José Ortega/Images.com*
Media Producer: *Shannon Gattens*
Media Project Manager: *Michele Borrelli*
Senior Production Supervisor: *Carol A. Bielski*
Composition: *Lachina Publishing Services*
Printing: *PMS Black, 50# Windsor Offset, Bookmart Press*

**Library of Congress Control Number: 2005922616**

The Internet addresses listed in the text were accurate at the time of publication. The inclusion of a
website does not indicate an endorsement by the authors of McGraw-Hill, and McGraw-Hill does not
guarantee the accuracy of the information presented at these sites.

www.mhhe.com

I've often thought there ought to be a manual to hand to little kids, telling them what kind of planet they're on, why they don't fall off, how much time they've probably got here, how to avoid poison ivy, and so on. . . . And one thing I would really like to tell them about is cultural relativity. I didn't learn until I was in college about all the other cultures, and I should have learned that in the first grade. A first grader should understand that his or her culture isn't a rational invention; that there are thousands of other cultures and they all work pretty well; that all cultures function on faith rather than truth; that there are lots of alternatives to our own society. Cultural relativity is defensible and attractive. It's also a source of hope. It means we don't have to continue this way if we don't like it.

—Kurt Vonnegut, 1974

This may be the start of that manual.

—Kenneth Cushner, 2006

# About the Author

Kenneth Cushner (Ed. D.) is Executive Director for International Affairs and Professor in the College and Graduate School of Education at Kent State University. He is a frequent contributor to the professional literature in multicultural and intercultural education and is internationally known for his work in the professional development of educators through workshops and consultation. Among his publications, Dr. Cushner is the author or co-author of *Human Diversity in Education: An Integrative Approach,* 5th ed. (McGraw-Hill, 2006); *Beyond Tourism: A Practical Guide to Meaningful Educational Travel* (Scarecrow Education, 2004); *International Perspectives on Intercultural Education* (Lawrence Erlbaum Associates, 1998); *Intercultural Interactions: A Practical Guide,* 2nd ed. (Sage Publications, 1996), and *Improving Intercultural Interactions: Modules for Cross-Cultural Training Programs, Volume 2* (Sage Publication, 1997). Dr. Cushner has developed and led international travel programs on all seven continents. In his spare time, Dr. Cushner enjoys music (percussion and guitar), travel, and photography.

# Table of Contents

## Part III    Modifying Curriculum and Instruction to Address the Goals of Diversity

# Preface

With the publication of the third edition of *Human Diversity in Action: Developing Multicultural Competencies for the Classroom,* we find people becoming increasingly interconnected and interdependent, both on the domestic front as well as across the globe. The smooth functioning of many governments, economies, and businesses increasingly requires more people to have greater awareness, knowledge, and skill in order to interact effectively with those whose cultures may be quite different from their own. It is increasingly clear that people must strive to better understand those who are culturally different as well as to make themselves better known to others. This will be no simple feat given what we know about the manner in which people learn about others.

## Why It Is Important to Use This Workbook

The fields of cross-cultural training and intercultural education continue to grow in response to these very real needs. One thing that stands out in the research of intercultural education and training is the critical role that meaningful experience plays in culture learning. That is, while it is relatively easy to transfer a significant amount of valid information to others through cognitive approaches such as lectures, books, and films, just having new information itself is not sufficient to make people behave any differently. Thus, typical multicultural courses that emphasize lecture and readings may fall far short of achieving the very goals they set out to accomplish; students and teachers just do not become more effective in their interpersonal interactions or in modifying their instruction simply by being presented with new information. Rather, people learn to live and work more effectively with others as a result of long-term immersion and active experiences that engage the emotions, and often precede or accompany cognitive inputs.

This workbook was developed with the intent of providing the student of culture with structured experiences designed to increase awareness, knowledge, and skill in intercultural understanding and interaction with the ultimate impact being on teachers and students in schools. Through this workbook, students and instructors can become actively engaged in many practical exercises that examine critical elements of the educational process that are influenced by culture. They can then discuss their experiences with others, gaining comfort with what are often difficult concepts and topics to speak about. Thus, users of this workbook benefit by reflection, dialogue, and collaboration.

## To the Instructor—Using the Workbook

This workbook will be useful to those teaching a variety of courses where culture and/or human diversity are central elements. People have found these exercises to be of value in such courses as multicultural, global or international education; social studies or other methods courses that require students to attend to diversity in very real ways; new student orientation courses that emphasize diversity issues; as well as in a variety of field experience settings, including student teaching seminars. This collection of activities can also be a very useful addition to the professional development of practicing teachers, providing the workshop consultant with a variety of activities designed to bring aspects of diversity to the forefront.

This workbook was designed to easily accompany our text *Human Diversity in Education: An Integrative Approach,* now in its 5th edition (Cushner, McClelland and Safford, McGraw-Hill ©2006), and the workbook activities are keyed directly in the text at appropriate points to alert students and instructors.

The workbook can also be used alone, or can easily be used as a complement to many of the multicultural textbooks currently available on the market. A correlation chart, housed on the workbook's Web site at www.mhhe.cushner3e, identifies where specific activities might be used in conjunction with some of the other multicultural textbooks that are in current use.

## To the Student—Why You Are Using This Workbook

It is important that you understand that you must be an active participant in your own learning if you are to truly understand diversity and issues surrounding culture. Culture learning is not effectively accomplished in a passive mode. Thus, this workbook is designed to be consumable, and is intended to be linked closely with the content you are reading about in your textbook. That is, you are encouraged to write in this workbook and to use the various exercises as guides to help you develop a more culturally sensitive approach to your interactions with others, and ultimately a more authentic approach to teaching and learning.

## The Organization of the Workbook

This workbook provides several exercises that are presented in three different sections, or levels of culture learning. Part I provides basic content related to the concept of culture and the development of self. It is essential that anyone seriously interested in exploring the complex phenomenon of culture and intercultural interaction look closely at the various dynamics that have gone into the formation of self. Part II provides basic frameworks and skills in the analysis of cultural differences and the processes involved in intercultural interaction. Part III presents exercises to provide insight into culture's influence on teaching and learning as well as a number of strategies that can be used to modify existing curriculum and instruction. You are encouraged to use these exercises over a relatively long period of time, such as throughout a semester or academic year, as the changes that we are all required to make, both within ourselves as well as within our institutions, are quite dramatic and will not happen overnight.

## New to This Edition of the Workbook

This workbook has been well received by previous users. Thus, this third edition follows a similar format as the previous editions. Previous users will, however, notice a few changes. There are fewer activities in this edition, thus making it easier to complete in the course of an academic term. Additional activities are available online at **www.mhhe.com/cushner3e**. Changes have been made to individual exercises and new activities have been included based on the feedback of current users.

## Acknowledgments

A project such as this cannot develop and improve without the insights and assistance of many individuals. To this end, the following individuals deserve thanks:

Charles Ervin, Florida A&M University
Lyn Froning, University of Alabama at Birmingham
Carolyn B. Hines, University of Southern Indiana
Regina M. Schaefer, University of La Verne
Ellie-Ann Shahinian Baldwin, Mesa State College
Howard Starks, Wayne State University
Gary Stiler, University of Southern Indiana
Anh Tran, Wichita State University
Kathleen Wheeler, York College

# *Online Resources for* Human Diversity in Action

www.mhhe.com/cushner3e

## Additional Readings and Activities

Online Activity 1: Interpreting One's Own Intercultural Experience: The Magic of Journal Writing

Online Activity and Reading 2: How Culture is Learned: Socializing Agents

Online Activity 3: Examining Stereotypes Held by Self and Others

Online Activity and Reading 4: The Triad Model for Developing Multicultural Understanding

Online Activity 5: Using the Interpersonal Cultural Grid to Expand Intercultural Understanding

## Additional Critical Incidents

## PowerWeb Articles and Newsfeeds

## Electronic Versions of Activities 2, 13, 14, 19, 30 and 36

## Related Web Links

Access to the above resources is free using the passcode card packaged with your new workbook. If you have a used workbook, you can purchase access at www.mhhe.com/cushner3e.

# part one

# Getting to Know the Culture of Self

# Mental Maps of Culture: An Icebreaker

## Purpose

1. To reflect upon your early experiences related to culture and intercultural interaction.

2. To learn about others as you each share and discuss your early experiences and understanding of the concept of culture.

## Instructions

Reflect upon some of the experiences you had growing up that may have influenced your understanding of the concept of culture. Perhaps you grew up in an environment that was filled with culturally diverse experiences and encounters. Or, perhaps you were raised in a rather segregated or protected environment and had little direct experience with people different from yourself. When did you first learn about different people? How did you react to this experience? What messages did others give you — either intentionally or not, that you still remember today? How have you come to understand the concept of culture today? Reflect back over your life and try to recall events and experiences along the way that have influenced your feelings and thoughts about people from different cultural backgrounds.

In the space below, or on another sheet of paper, make a drawing or diagram that includes your experiences and your thoughts, feelings, and understanding related to culture. Then, using your drawing, introduce yourself to one or two other people while sharing your experiences with culture. In your discussion, look for similarities and differences in your feelings and thoughts, the events and experiences that contributed to their development, and the people who influenced you along the way.

# Inventory of Cross-Cultural Sensitivity

## Purpose

To complete a self-assessment instrument regarding your intercultural experiences.

## Instructions

The following questionnaire asks you to rate your agreement or disagreement with a series of statements. Please respond honestly as there are no correct answers. You will find another copy of this in the last section of the workbook that you can complete at a later time. You can compare your responses from the beginning to the end of the book.

Please circle the number that best corresponds to your level of agreement with each statement below

| | *1 = Strongly Disagree    7 = Strongly Agree* |
|---|---|
| 1. I speak only one language | 1...2...3...4...5...6...7 |
| 2. The way other people express themselves is very interesting to me | 1...2...3...4...5...6...7 |
| 3. I enjoy being with people from other cultures | 1...2...3...4...5...6...7 |
| 4. Foreign influence in our country threatens our national identity | 1...2...3...4...5...6...7 |
| 5. Others' feelings rarely influence decisions I make | 1...2...3...4...5...6...7 |
| 6. I cannot eat with chopsticks | 1...2...3...4...5...6...7 |
| 7. I avoid people who are different from me | 1...2...3...4...5...6...7 |
| 8. It is better that people from other cultures avoid one another | 1...2...3...4...5...6...7 |
| 9. Culturally mixed marriages are wrong | 1...2...3...4...5...6...7 |
| 10. I think people are basically alike | 1...2...3...4...5...6...7 |
| 11. I have never lived outside my own culture for any great length of time | 1...2...3...4...5...6...7 |

| | *1 = Strongly Disagree    7 = Strongly Agree* |
|---|---|
| 12. I have foreigners to my home on a regular basis | 1...2...3...4...5...6...7 |
| 13. It makes me nervous to talk to people who are different from me | 1...2...3...4...5...6...7 |
| 14. I enjoy studying about people from other cultures | 1...2...3...4...5...6...7 |
| 15. People from other cultures do things differently because they do not know any other way | 1...2...3...4...5...6...7 |
| 16. There is usually more than one good way to get things done | 1...2...3...4...5...6...7 |
| 17. I listen to music from another culture on a regular basis | 1...2...3...4...5...6...7 |
| 18. I decorate my home or room with artifacts from other countries | 1...2...3...4...5...6...7 |
| 19. I feel uncomfortable when in a crowd of people | 1...2...3...4...5...6...7 |
| 20. The very existence of humanity depends on our knowledge about other people | 1...2...3...4...5...6...7 |
| 21. Residential neighborhoods should be culturally separated | 1...2...3...4...5...6...7 |
| 22. I have many friends | 1...2...3...4...5...6...7 |
| 23. I dislike eating foods from other cultures | 1...2...3...4...5...6...7 |
| 24. I think about living within another culture in the future | 1...2...3...4...5...6...7 |
| 25. Moving into another culture would be easy | 1...2...3...4...5...6...7 |
| 26. I like to discuss issues with people from other cultures | 1...2...3...4...5...6...7 |
| 27. There should be tighter controls on the number of immigrants allowed into my country | 1...2...3...4...5...6...7 |
| 28. The more I know about people, the more I dislike them | 1...2...3...4...5...6...7 |
| 29. I read more national news than international news in the daily newspaper | 1...2...3...4...5...6...7 |
| 30. Crowds of foreigners frighten me | 1...2...3...4...5...6...7 |
| 31. When something newsworthy happens I seek out someone from that part of the world to discuss the issue with | 1...2...3...4...5...6...7 |
| 32. I eat ethnic foods at least twice a week | 1...2...3...4...5...6...7 |

## Scoring the ICCS

The ICCS can be scored by subscales. Simply insert the number circled on the test form in the spaces provided under each subscale heading. Reverse the values for the items marked with an asterisk (*). For instance, reverse scoring results in:

$$7=1, 6=2, 5=3, 4=4, 3=5, 2=6, 1=7$$

Then, add the values in each column for the subscale score. A total ICCS score is obtained by adding the various subscale scores together. Individuals can be ranked relative to others in a particular group. You can also identify relative strengths and weaknesses that may lead to more focused orientation and planning.

ICCS Scoring Guide    Subject ID_____

| C Scale | | B Scale | | I Scale | |
|---|---|---|---|---|---|
| *item* | *score* | *item* | *score* | *item* | *score* |
| 1* | ____ | 2 | ____ | 3 | ____ |
| 6* | ____ | 7* | ____ | 8* | ____ |
| 11* | ____ | 13* | ____ | 14 | ____ |
| 12 | ____ | 19* | ____ | 20 | ____ |
| 17 | ____ | 25* | ____ | 26 | ____ |
| 18 | ____ | 30 | ____ | 31 | ____ |
| 23* | ____ | | | | |
| 24 | ____ | | | | |
| 29* | ____ | | | | |
| 32 | ____ | | | | |

| | A Scale | | E Scale | |
|---|---|---|---|---|
| | *item* | *score* | *item* | *score* |
| | 4* | ____ | 5* | ____ |
| | 9* | ____ | 10 | ____ |
| | 15* | ____ | 16 | ____ |
| | 21* | ____ | 22 | ____ |
| | 27* | ____ | 28* | ____ |

*Totals*

C Scale = ____

B Scale = ____

I Scale = ____

A Scale = ____

E Scale = ____

Total ICCS Score = ____

* Reverse score all items marked with * as these are negatively worded items.

## Interpreting the Inventory of Cross-Cultural Sensitivity

The ICCS is a 32-item instrument that provides dimensional scores for individuals on each of five subscales. Individuals can be ranked relative to others from high to low levels of sensitivity on issues and experiences related to cross-cultural or intercultural interaction (the higher the score, the more sensitive an individual is presumed to be). While the ICCS should not be used in a predictive manner, results can be used to raise people's awareness of some of the issues to consider prior to intercultural interaction. (The technical details of the ICCS can be found following the ICCS in Part 3.)

The five subscales and the range of scores include:

| Subscale | Range of Scores |
| --- | --- |
| Cultural Integration (C Scale): assesses the degree to which an individual integrates elements from cultures other than their own into their daily activities. | 10–70 |
| Behavioral Scale (B Scale): assesses the degree to which an individual has adopted behavior that is new or has a degree of comfort when interacting with others. | 6–42 |
| Intellectual Interaction (I Scale): assesses the degree to which an individual seeks out knowledge of other cultural orientations. | 6–42 |
| Attitude Toward Others (A Scale): assesses the degree of openness toward others. | 5–35 |
| Empathy Scale (E Scale): assesses the degree to which an individual identifies with the feelings of others | 5–35 |
| Total Score Range | 32–224 |

In which areas are you strongest? Weakest?

_____

_____

_____

What are some things you might do in order to increase your abilities in each of the dimensions of the scale?

_____

_____

_____

_____

# The Nature of Culture and Culture Learning

## Purpose

To identify qualities that characterize the concept of culture.

## Instructions

Read and review the following material. Respond accordingly in the space provided using examples from your own life.

The process by which people come to believe that there is a "right" way to think, express themselves, and act — in other words, how people learn their culture, is called **socialization**. It is the process by which individuals learn what is required of them in order to be successful members of a given group, whatever that group may be. Socialization is such a potent process that people are hardly aware that other realities can exist. The result is **ethnocentrism**, the tendency people have to judge others from their own culture's perspective, believing theirs to be the "right" or "correct" way to perceive and act within the world.

Most people in today's industrialized societies can be considered to be multicultural because they have been socialized by a number of different individuals or groups that influence their behavior and thought patterns (e.g., gender, nationality, ethnicity, social class, religion, and so forth). At this point, it may be helpful to look at how culture, in the broadest sense, influences people's behavior. Brislin (2000) and Cushner and Brislin (1996) offer a discussion of features that are helpful in understanding culture's influence on behavior and that can be applied to the multiple influences suggested above. This list is summarized below. You should consider each, and then apply it to your own lives and experiences with the various groups with which you interact. First, individually identify examples from your own past that reflect *each* of the aspects of culture. Then, share your responses in small groups. Be ready to share an example of each aspect with the larger group.

1. Culture usually refers to something that is made by human beings rather than something that occurs in nature. Thus, while sand along a beach may be a natural occurrence, the condominiums along the beachfront are not.

   My example:

   _____

   _____

   _____

   _____

2. Culture concerns itself with people's assumptions about life that are often unspoken or hidden from consciousness. Thus, most Americans, when putting a hand out to greet someone new, assume they will do likewise and then can shake hands. This may not be the case when meeting someone from Japan.

   My example of an aspect of my culture that I believe is "hidden" or a "secret":

   _____

   _____

   _____

   _____

3. Culture is a collective creation that most members of the group practice. In the United States, as well as many other countries, it is common for people to unconsciously walk on the right side of a hallway or sidewalk. In other countries, such as Britain, Australia or New Zealand, it is common for people to walk on the left side of hallways and sidewalks.

   My example of something most people from my cultural group practice that might be different from another group:

   _____

   _____

   _____

4. There exist clear childhood experiences that individuals can identify that help to develop and teach particular values and practices. For instance, the American value of individualism is often introduced to young people through early jobs they may have had (paper routes, babysitting, etc.).

My example of something I did in my childhood that teaches a cultural value or practice:

_____

_____

_____

_____

5. Because culture is often a secret and most people do not share a common vocabulary and understanding, people are often unable to comfortably discuss cross-cultural problems with others. Thus, cultural differences become most evident in well-meaning clashes.

My example of a culture clash that occurred because people did not understand the differing cultural perspectives that were operating at the time:

_____

_____

_____

_____

6. Culture allows people to fill in the blanks so they do not have to repeat the rules for every action to other members of the group. Thus, when someone is invited to a happy hour after work, it is clear to most people that they should expect to spend no more than a couple of hours at the bar or pub, and not plan to make a night of it.

My example of a common behavior that seems mostly automatic and commonly understood:

_____

_____

_____

_____

7. People experience strong emotional reactions when their cultural values are violated or when a culture's expected behaviors are ignored. Thus, recent rulings in France that students' heads must remain uncovered in school has drawn strong criticism from the Islamic community.

My example of a strong emotional response I have observed when people's cultures clash:

_____

_____

_____

_____

8. When changes in cultural values are contemplated, like legalizing same-sex marriages or outlawing the right of citizens to carry handguns, the reaction that "this will be a difficult uphill battle" is likely.

My example of a major cultural change that is or was difficult for people to make:

_____

_____

_____

_____

# Childhood Experiences

## Purpose

To identify early socialization experiences that have influenced one's cultural values, beliefs, and practices held today.

## Instructions

In order for culture to be a shared phenomenon it must be effectively transmitted to the young. Recall example 4 in Activity 3, *There exist clear childhood experiences that individuals can identify that help to develop and teach particular values and practices.* Identify three examples of cultural beliefs, values, and practices that are expected of "successful" representatives of American culture (or another culture with which you are familiar). Your list will include desirable beliefs, values, and behaviors.

| Beliefs | Values | Behaviors |
|---------|--------|-----------|
| _____ | _____ | _____ |
| _____ | _____ | _____ |
| _____ | _____ | _____ |

Next, consider an example from each column. What childhood experiences did you have that may have helped you to develop the cultural traits that are expected of you? (For instance, a paper route helps one develop responsibility, individuality, business sense, initiative, and so forth.) Describe early childhood experiences that may have helped you to achieve the desired and expected outcome.

_____

_____

_____

_____

_____

_____

# Understanding Cultural Complexity

## Purpose

To help you identify the complex and rather broad manner in which people use the concept 'culture.'

## Instructions

Review the following material and respond accordingly at each section.

The definition of cultural diversity that is most useful given the time and circumstances in which we live encompasses not only those individuals whose ethnic or cultural heritage originates in another country, but also those among us who have been socialized by different groups, those who may have special educational and other needs (e.g., those who are deaf), those who may share significantly different lifestyles (e.g., rural and urban children, people who live in extreme poverty), those who are significantly influenced by variations in class and religion, and so forth. In other words, culture is a very broad term, and in many ways, by this definition, everyone in a pluralistic society such as the United States, Canada, Australia, New Zealand, Great Britain, Israel, and so on can be considered, to some degree, multicultural.

The Deaf population is often used as an example of a group that has developed a unique culture with both subjective (invisible) and objective (observable) elements. People often think of deaf persons as being just like persons who can hear, except that they sign instead of speak. In most situations, this is not the case; the Deaf community has a culture specific to its members. Speech, for instance, is not valued, and is often considered inappropriate. Most people who are deaf do not sign Standard English (e.g., put signs together in Standard English word order) except when signing with hearing people. When interacting with other deaf people, American Sign Language (ASL), which has its own syntax, is used.

Accompanying the use of a distinct language among the Deaf population are patterns of behavior that are particular to the group, including some early childhood socialization practices. Children of deaf parents may grow up in environments with much greater visual orientation — lights may accompany a ringing telephone or doorbell, or people may depend upon gestures in interpersonal communication. The Deaf community is also very tightly knit, placing strong emphasis on social and family ties.

Eighty to ninety percent of people who are hearing-impaired marry others with hearing losses. Thus, a strong in-group orientation develops, making it difficult for outsiders who do not know ASL to enter.

Interactions between hearing and Deaf populations are often filled with feelings of anxiety, uncertainty, and a threat of loss—feelings that are all similar to those encountered in other intercultural exchanges. Using this as an example, it is easy to see the range of possible intercultural interactions that can occur between individuals and groups that have distinct subjective cultures.

The field of cross-cultural psychology offers educators the following set of ideas or principles that can be used to study the complexity of culture in schools and communities as well as in the classroom (Pedersen, 2000).

### 1. People tend to communicate their cultural identity to others in the broadest possible terms.

For instance, upon meeting someone for the first time you may communicate many different things about yourself; including your age, nationality, ethnic group, religious affiliation, where you grew up, and the nature of your family. At other times you may describe your status at work or in the community, your health, your social class, or the way you have come to understand your gender. In other words, people often share such things as demographic information, ethnographic information, as well as information about their status and various affiliations. Each of these sources of cultural identity carries with it associated rules for behavior. We offer such information to new acquaintances because by doing so we give them cultural clues regarding what to expect from us and how to interact with us.

People, thus, have multiple "cultures" influencing them at various times: their nationality, ethnicity, religion, and gender, to name just a few. Each and every one of us may be considered multicultural. It might be helpful for people to consider themselves to be composed of hundreds of different cultural influences.

What are some of the significant forces in your life that you can identify at this time? Try to identify *at least* three different cultural influences that guide your behavior and thinking. Then tell how each influences you.

| Cultural Influence | How It Guides Me |
|---|---|
| _____ | _____ |
| _____ | _____ |
| _____ | _____ |
| _____ | _____ |
| _____ | _____ |
| _____ | _____ |

**2. Culture is not static, either in the individual or in the group. One's cultural identity is dynamic and always changing.**

As our environmental circumstances and group associations change, we adapt our cultural identity and behavior patterns accordingly. In certain circumstances our gender-related knowledge and beliefs may be predominant; at another time our religious beliefs may be most evident; and at still other times our ethnicity may be at the forefront. Thus, our own multicultural nature leads to behavior variations that are sometimes difficult to understand and appreciate.

Consider two situations you have experienced when distinctly different cultural forces influenced your thoughts and/or actions.

_____

_____

_____

**3. Culture is complex, but it is not chaotic. Good students of culture look for patterns in people's behavior. When these patterns are understood, the complexity that was perceived at first can be better understood.**

Culture helps individuals make sense of their world and, thereby, to develop more routine in their behavior to fit different environments. Common phrases such as the "culture of the organization," "the culture of the community," or the "culture of the society" refer to the fact that culture is not simply patterned for an individual, but also for a setting, a community, or a society as a whole. When viewed from the outside, these patterns can at first appear quite complicated and difficult to understand. Yet each of us moves quite easily among the many different cultural patterns with which we are familiar. When confronted by someone whose behavior is *not* familiar it is the responsibility of the outsider to listen, to observe, and to inquire closely so that the patterns of that person (or social group, or society) become evident and understood. To do so decreases the possibility of misunderstanding and conflict, and increases the likelihood that new and useful understanding and appreciation will be gained.

Try to identify a situation with which you are familiar where different patterns of expectations and behavior are evident. In what ways do these patterns differ from other similar contexts with which you are familiar (for instance, you may be aware that the Jewish celebration for the New Year is different from the Christian celebration). Briefly describe this context to the best of your ability.

**Example**:

_____

_____

_____

_____

**4. Interactions with other cultures can be viewed as a resource for learning.**
Culturally different encounters help to prepare individuals to deal more effectively with the complexity that is increasingly a part of life. That, in essence, is one of the major goals of an education that is multicultural—for people to become more complex thinkers, bring more insights into various situations, and thus be more accurate in their interpretations of others' behavior. In short, the number of cultural variables we learn to accommodate will determine our ability to navigate within a fast-moving, ever-changing society.

Tell of an occasion where you interacted with someone from another culture. What do you think you learned about that group as a result of your interaction? How certain are you that your knowledge is accurate?

**Interaction:**

_____

_____

_____

**What I learned:**

_____

_____

_____

_____

**Is my knowledge accurate?**

_____

_____

_____

_____

**5. Behavior should be judged in relation to its context.**

This means that observable behavior cannot be understood apart from the context in which it occurs. Seen outside its context, another's "different" behavior can, at best, seem meaningless, and, at worst, be profoundly misinterpreted. Contextual inquiry allows us to be accurate in our judgments of others.

Consider this example of a particularly troublesome 11-year-old boy who would become rowdy and disruptive in the classroom every day about 2:00 in the afternoon. Inevitably, the teacher sent the child to the office where, because it was late in the day, he was promptly sent home. Defined in terms of the middle-class cultural context of the school, this was definitely a troubled child, and he was so labeled by nearly all the adults in the building. Eventually, an astute counselor recognized a pattern and did some inquiry. It turned out that the mother's boyfriend came home every day about 2:45, oftentimes quite drunk and abusive. In his rage, the boyfriend frequently abused the mother. The boy, quite accurately understanding the cultural patterns of the school and the home, figured out that his misbehavior would result in his being sent home, and that if he was sent home by 2:30, he would arrive before the boyfriend and thus be able to protect his mother. Suddenly our so-called troubled boy's behavior makes sense and he becomes something of a hero because he found a way to protect his vulnerable mother. Again, without full knowledge of the context, behavior is often meaningless or badly misinterpreted.

Give an example of an instance where you initially misunderstood something that was going on. How did you come to finally understand that the situation was different from how it initially appeared?

_____

_____

_____

_____

_____

_____

**6. Persons holding a multicultural perspective continually strive to find common ground between individuals.**

In a sense, we must strive to be cross-eyed. That is, we must be able to see the similarities among people as well as their differences. While it is the differences that tend to stand out and separate people, it is precisely in our similarities where common ground, or a common meeting point, can be found. A multicultural perspective allows two people to disagree without either being wrong. In other words, dialogue between people can continue, which is a key to furthering cross-cultural understanding and mediating differences between people. In this view, cultural differences become tolerable and an "us-them" or a "we-they" debate is avoided. There are no winners and losers. We are all in this together. Either we all win or we all lose.

Give an example of a compromise you are aware of. What common ground was found between the two parties? How was the common ground established?

# Proverbs as a Window into One's Culture

## Purpose

1. To examine proverbs as a reflection of culture.

2. To explore the influence of American mainstream values on behavior and educational practice.

3. To compare mainstream values with those of other groups.

## Instructions

Generating a list of proverbs you have grown up with is an excellent way to explore underlying values that may guide your own behavior. This proverbs exercise has three components:

1. Generate a list of proverbs that you recall hearing as you grew up or that influence you today.
2. Identify what underlying value is expressed by the proverb.
3. State how this value or belief might influence your beliefs and behavior as a teacher.

In small groups, try to find *at least* four proverbs for which you can complete all three parts. Groups should be as homogeneous as possible (e.g., all males or females; separated by ethnicity; etc.). Subsequent group discussions can then consider culture-specific experiences. For instance:

*Proverb*

The early bird catches the worm.

*Underlying Value*

Initiative

*Influence on Education*

A person holding this value might more readily take advantage of the educational opportunities provided to him or her.

*Proverb*

_____

_____

_____


*Underlying Value*

_____

_____

_____


*Influence on Education*

_____

_____

_____


*Proverb*

_____

_____

_____


*Underlying Value*

_____

_____

_____


*Influence on Education*

_____

_____

_____

*Proverb*

_____

_____

_____

*Underlying Value*

_____

_____

_____

*Influence on Education*

_____

_____

_____

*Proverb*

_____

_____

_____

*Underlying Value*

_____

_____

_____

*Influence on Education*

_____

_____

_____

## Proverbs: A Cross-Cultural Survey

Following are examples of proverbs from other cultures. Consider some of these, and in small groups discuss what you think the underlying value might be and examples of proverbs from your own culture that you believe are similar.

### African

He who sows nettles does not reap roses.
A horse that arrives early gets good drinking water.
By trying often, the monkey learns to jump from the tree.
Little by little grow the bananas.
It takes a village to raise a child.

### African American

You got eyes to see and wisdom not to see.
Muddy roads call the milepost a liar.
Every bell ain't a dinner bell.
The graveyard is the cheapest boarding house.

### Arabic

An empty drum makes a big sound.
If you take off clothes you are naked. If you take away family, you are nothing.
Doing things quickly is from the devil.
If you want to know somebody, look at her or his friends.
Do not stand in a place of danger trusting in miracles.
Live together like brothers and do business like strangers.

### Canadian

Don't sell the bearskin before you kill the bear.

### Chinese

Ice three feet thick isn't frozen in a day.
If one plants melons, one gets melons.
The plan of the year is in the spring. The plan of the day is in the morning. The plan of life is in hardship.
Be not afraid of growing slowly, be afraid only of standing still.
Talk doesn't cook rice.

## German

Joy, moderation, and rest shut out the doctors.

Young gambler, old beggar.

## Indian

I grumbled that I had no shoes until I saw a man who had no feet.

With every rising of the sun think of your life as just begun.

Call on God, but row away from the rocks.

## Israeli

Keep a small head.

If you're clever, keep silent.

Life is not a picnic.

Light is not recognized except through darkness.

Don't spit into the well — you might drink from it later.

God could not be everywhere and therefore he made mothers.

A half-truth is a whole lie.

Don't be too sweet lest you be eaten up; don't be too bitter lest you be spewed out.

## Italian

He who knows little quickly tells it.

Once the game is over, the king and the pawn go back in the same box.

He who knows nothing doubts nothing.

## Japanese

You will gain three moons if you wake early in the morning.

Even monkeys fall from trees.

You can't get clams from a field.

Too many skippers bring the boat to the mountain.

Fall seven times, stand up eight.

Fast ripe, fast rotten.

The reverse side also has a reverse side.

## Mexican

To win a dispute is to gain a chicken and lose a cow.

True friendship is one soul shared by two bodies.

Of doctor and poet, musician and madman, we each have a trace.

The sun is the blanket of the poor.

### Native American

After dark all cats are leopards. (Zuni)

Do not wrong or hate your neighbor for it is not he that you wrong but yourself.
(Pima)

Every animal knows more than you do. (Nez Perce)

It is less of a problem to be poor than to be dishonest. (Anishinabe)

A rocky vineyard does not need a prayer, but a pick ax. (Navajo)

We will be known forever by the tracks we leave. (Dakota)

Those that lie down with dogs, get up with fleas. (Blackfoot)

### Polish

Fish, to taste good, must swim three times: in water, in butter, and in wine.

The greater love is a mother's; then comes a dog's; then a sweetheart's.

Do not push the river, it will flow by itself.

A good painter need not give a name to his picture, a bad one must.

Even a clock that does not work is right twice a day.

A guest sees more in an hour than the host in a year.

### Russian

Every peasant is proud of the pond in his village because from it he measures
the sea.

Every road has two directions.

The hammer shatters glass but forges steel.

He who doesn't risk will never get to drink champagne.

Ask a lot, but take what is offered.

### Spanish

One bird in the hand is worth one thousand flying.

Your getting up early doesn't make the sun rise earlier.

Don't speak unless you can improve on the silence.

From a fallen tree, all make kindling.

If your house is on fire, warm yourself by it.

# Cultural Values in American Society

## Purpose

To explore the relationship between cultural values and their expression in institutions, especially the American school, and to consider how some of these values may be changing.

## Instructions

Read the following discussion of traditional American values. Then, respond to the questions according to how you see the particular value expressed in society.

American culture is complex, and many would say that it is difficult to identify a national culture or what might be called "typical" American cultural patterns. Many European Americans, for instance, think of themselves as having no culture, as being citizens of a nation too young to have really developed a culture. Nothing, however, could be further from the truth. Every group of people with any history has created a culture that pervades their thoughts and actions. American society is rich with diverse cultural patterns that, for many, come together in the schools. Since cultural patterns associated with the European American middle class have provided the foundation in most schools in this society, these patterns will be analyzed in terms of the school experience and school readiness. You should be making comparisons to other groups within American society.

A brief reflection on American history suggests that those who colonized North America had relatively weak ties to their homelands. The extended family, important in the country of origin, was separated, leaving the nuclear family as the predominant source of strength and identity. This had a tremendous influence on the development of the "American" character, since people's orientation had to shift from the larger collective to the individual or nuclear family unit. It is here that we see the beginnings of an individualistic orientation. In addition, as people came to settle the United States, the need to adjust to uncertainty, as well as to focus on change and development for survival, became paramount. Many of these values are in conflict with those held in many ethnic communities today.

Over the years, a dominant European American middle-class culture emerged that rests on six major values. In the previous exercise you explored values by looking at proverbs and sayings that have become a part of our folk wisdom. Since such proverbs express the values of a people, they are an excellent indicator of the folk-knowledge that supports and integrates society.

Reflect upon each mainstream value presented below and how it has influenced schools. Then, try to identify where another group's cultural value might be in support or conflict with it. If you represent a non-American culture, what values are reflected in your home society? Then, respond to similar questions.

---

*1. European Americans have a tendency to view themselves as separate from nature and able to master or control their environment.*

As a result, a high value is placed on science and technology as the predominant means of interacting with the world. This results in objectivity, rationality, materialism, and a need for concrete evidence. Proverbs and sayings such as "Necessity is the mother of invention," and "We'll cross that bridge when we come to it" reflect this belief.

---

How do you see this value expressed in society?

_____

_____

_____

How do you see this value expressed in schools?

_____

_____

_____

Can you identify a cultural group whose values might be in conflict with this one? Support your response.

_____

_____

_____

Do you have any indication that this value is undergoing change in recent years? If so, please explain.

_____

_____

_____

> ### 2. European Americans are action-oriented.
>
> As with number 1, this results in measurable accomplishments and an emphasis on efficiency and practicality. Progress and change thus become important concepts. Our schools expect such an orientation, as evidenced by an emphasis on testing and measurement as well as a nearly religious belief in the efficiency of paperwork assignments. Proverbs such as "Seeing is believing," and "The proof is in the pudding" emphasize this cultural trait.

How do you see this value expressed in society?

_____

_____

_____

How do you see this value expressed in schools?

_____

_____

_____

Can you identify a cultural group whose values might be in conflict with this one? Support your response.

_____

_____

_____

Do you have any indication that this value is undergoing change in recent years? If so, please explain.

_____

_____

_____

> **3. European Americans have a future orientation; they believe in the promise that things will be bigger and better.**
>
> Most middle-class European Americans are seldom content with the present; they wish not to be considered old-fashioned, and they believe that effort applied in the present will affect their future. Progress is, in many ways, their most important product. Proverbs such as "I think I can, I think I can," and "A penny saved is a penny earned," reflect this tendency.

How do you see this value expressed in society?

_____

_____

_____

How do you see this value expressed in schools?

_____

_____

_____

Can you identify a cultural group whose values might be in conflict with this one? Support your response.

_____

_____

_____

_____

Do you have any indication that this value is undergoing change in recent years? If so, please explain.

_____

_____

_____

> **4. European Americans are self-motivated and comfortable setting their own goals and directions.**
>
> From an early age, the majority of European Americans are encouraged to reach out on their own, to attempt for themselves, to satisfy their own needs. Such proverbs as "Nothing ventured, nothing gained," "If at first you don't succeed, try, try again," and "The early bird catches the worm," reflect this trait.

How do you see this value expressed in society?

_____

_____

_____

How do you see this value expressed in schools?

_____

_____

_____

Can you identify a cultural group whose values might be in conflict with this one? Support your response.

_____

_____

_____

Do you have any indication that this value is undergoing change in recent years? If so, please explain.

_____

_____

_____

*5. European Americans have a strong sense of individuality.*

The belief that the "self" as an individual is separate from others results in a tendency to emphasize individual initiative, independence, action, and interests. From an early age, children are encouraged to make their own decisions and to develop their individual skills and abilities, and in the traditional school, children are expected to work alone in their seats, rarely coming together for group work. Proverbs such as "Too many cooks spoil the broth," "Don't judge a book by its cover," and "God helps those who help themselves" stress this value.

How do you see this value expressed in society?

_____

_____

_____

How do you see this value expressed in schools?

_____

_____

_____

Can you identify a cultural group whose values might be in conflict with this one? Support your response.

_____

_____

_____

_____

Do you have any indication that this value is undergoing change in recent years? If so, please explain.

_____

_____

_____

**6. Finally, European Americans believe in the mutability of human nature.**

This belief, that it is relatively easy to change and that a cultural environment can mold people, underlies the assimilationist ideology that has pervaded American public education for so many years. "A stranger is only a friend you haven't met yet," and "Leaders are made, not born" may reflect this notion.

How do you see this value expressed in society?

_____

_____

_____

How do you see this value expressed in schools?

_____

_____

_____

Can you identify a cultural group whose values might be in conflict with this one? Support your response.

_____

_____

_____

Do you have any indication that this value is undergoing change in recent years? If so, please explain.

_____

_____

_____

# Family Tree: Tracing One's Roots and Family Experiences

## Purpose

To discover your family's experiences in past generations and compare them with those of immigrants and refugees today.

## Instructions

Respond to the reflective questions below.

Most people in the United States can trace their family history, or roots, to someplace other than where they currently reside. Speak with family members and look through old family photographs (if you have any) to trace your family's heritage as far back as possible. If you were adopted or do not know your ancestors, respond in terms of an adoptive or foster family, or one with which you closely identify. Respond to the following questions as best you can and share your responses with others.

**From what parts of the world did your family (or families) originate?**

_____

_____

_____


**What motivated your ancestors to leave their homeland for a New World? When did they leave? If your ancestors were always in North America, what was their life like prior to European contact?**

_____

_____

_____

**What hardships did your ancestors face in previous generations, either when they first arrived or soon after contact? What did they do to overcome any hardships? Do they recall any prejudice that was experienced?**

_____

_____

_____

**What did your ancestors do in the previous two or three generations? How did this influence what the family does today?**

_____

_____

_____

_____

_____

**What languages did your ancestors speak? What has happened to these languages in your family today?**

_____

_____

_____

_____

_____

**What family traditions or practices have been performed over the years that are special or unique to your family?**

_____

_____

_____

_____

What do you know of the meaning behind your family name? How, if at all, has it changed over the years? Do you know the reason for any changes?

_____

_____

_____

_____

_____

How are the experiences of your family similar to or different from those faced by various immigrants or refugees today?

_____

_____

_____

_____

_____

In what ways was this exercise easy or difficult for you to do? Under what circumstances might an exercise like this be difficult for a student to do? What might you do as a teacher to modify it in special circumstances?

_____

_____

_____

_____

_____

## Activity 9

# Who Am I?

### Purpose

To generate a list reflecting the categories with which you identify.

### Instructions

Complete the statement, "I am a(n) ___," rather quickly 20 times in the spaces provided below. Do not think too long about your responses as no answers are right or wrong.

1.  I am a(n) _____.
2.  I am a(n) _____.
3.  I am a(n) _____.
4.  I am a(n) _____.
5.  I am a(n) _____.
6.  I am a(n) _____.
7.  I am a(n) _____.
8.  I am a(n) _____.
9.  I am a(n) _____.
10. I am a(n) _____.
11. I am a(n) _____.
12. I am a(n) _____.
13. I am a(n) _____.
14. I am a(n) _____.
15. I am a(n) _____.
16. I am a(n) _____.
17. I am a(n) _____.
18. I am a(n) _____.
19. I am a(n) _____.
20. I am a(n) _____.

When you have finished, divide your responses according to the underlying categories you are able to recognize. This strategy can help you gain a picture of the image you have of yourself.

How many entries represent individual
traits (singer, dancer, student, for instance)?                    _____

How many entries represent collective
affiliations (member of a choir or
dance company, for instance)?                                        _____

Ethnic group identification is often used to describe human groups who share a common historical heritage, a sense of peoplehood, or the feeling that one's own destiny is somehow linked with that of others.

How early on your list did ethnic identity appear?        _____

What does its placement suggest about you and your identity with an ethnic group? If it appeared toward the bottom of the list, to what do you attribute this? If it appeared toward the top of the list, to what do you attribute this? If it did not appear at all, to what do you attribute this?

_____

_____

_____

What would you miss if your ethnicity were taken away from you?

_____

_____

_____

_____

Compare your responses with those of others in your class. Discuss the relative number of individualistic versus collective references on your list. How does the placement of your ethnic-group identity relate to the number of individualistic or collective identifications on your list? What might this mean about the importance of ethnicity to some people?

_____

_____

_____

_____

_____

_____

_____

_____

_____

_____

_____

_____

_____

_____

_____

_____

_____

_____

# The Culture Learning Process

*The following is further expanded upon in Human Diversity in Education: An Integrative Approach, 5th ed., 2006, Kenneth Cushner, Averil McClelland, and Philip Safford*

## Purpose

To identify the results of major socializing influences on your life.

## Instructions

As suggested earlier, individuals tend to identify themselves in a broad manner and in terms of many physical and social attributes. For example, a young man might identify himself as an attractive, athletic, Asian American who intends to be a doctor and live in upper-class society. It is important to note that others also identify individuals according to these attributes and that interactions among individuals are often shaped by such identifications. Incorporated into Figure 10-1 are twelve such attributes or manifestations of culture that researchers suggest influence teaching and learning. Who learns what, how, and when it is learned will be briefly described below. You will be asked to examine yourself in regard to each of these attributes.

## What Is Learned: The Attributes of Culture

### Race

Biologically speaking, race refers to the clustering of inherited physical characteristics that favor adaptation to a particular ecological area. However, race is culturally defined in the sense that different societies emphasize different sets of physical characteristics when referring to the same race. In fact, the term is so imprecise that it has even been used to refer to a wide variety of categories that are not physical, such as linguistic categories (the *English-speaking* race), religious categories (the *Jewish* race), national categories (the *Italian* race), and even to somewhat mythological categories (the *Teutonic* race). Although race has often been defined as a biological category, it has been argued that race as a biological concept is of little use because there are no "pure" races. Recent research in mapping the genetic code of five people of different races demonstrates that the concept of race has no scientific basis (*Akron Beacon Journal,* 2000). In the United States, race is judged largely on the basis of skin color, which some people consider very meaningful and use as a criterion for extending or withholding privileges of various kinds. Racism results from the transformation of race prejudice and/or ethnocentrism through the exercise of power against a racial group defined as inferior, by individuals

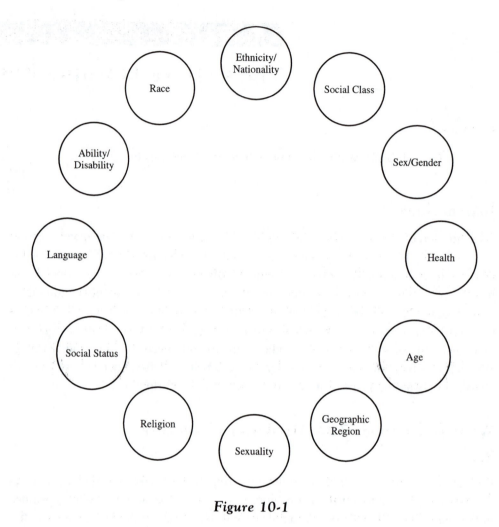

*Figure 10-1*

or institutions, with the intentional or unintentional support of an entire culture. Simply stated, preference for or belief in the superiority of one own racial group might be called racism.

**How is race evident in your life?**

_____

_____

_____

_____

## Sex/Gender

Sex is culturally defined on the basis of a particular set of physical characteristics. In this case, however, the characteristics are related to male and female reproduction. Cultural meanings associated with gender are expressed in terms of socially valued behaviors (e.g., nurturing the young and providing food) that are assigned according to sex. Such culturally assigned behaviors eventually become so accepted that they are thought of as natural for that sex. Thus, gender is what it *means* to be male or female in a society, and gender roles are those sets of behaviors thought by a particular people to be "normal" and "good" when performed by the assigned sex.

**How is sex/gender evident in your life?**

_____

_____

_____

_____

## Health

Health is culturally defined according to a particular group's view of what physical, mental, and emotional states constitute a "healthy" person. The "expert" opinion of the medical profession usually guides a society's view of health. Although a medical model has dominated cultural definitions of health in Western societies, most disabilities (mental retardation, deafness, blindness, etc.) are not judged in terms of this model's norms. Thus it is possible to be a healthy blind person or a healthy person with mental retardation. Nor would a person with cerebral palsy be considered "sick."

In the United States and most of the industrialized world, the prevailing health system is almost totally biomedical. However, alternative systems such as acupuncture, holistic medicine, and faith healing are available, and the acceptance of alternative systems varies widely both within and between social groups.

**How is health evident in your life?**

_____

_____

_____

_____

## *Ability/Disability*

As with definitions of health, ability and disability are culturally defined according to society's view about what it means to be physically, emotionally, and mentally "able." The categories of "ability" and "disability" refer to a wide variety of mental and physical characteristics: intelligence, emotional stability, impairment of sensory and neural systems, and impairment of movement. The social significance of these characteristics may vary by setting as well. For example, the terms "learning disability" or "learning disabled" are terms primarily used with reference to schooling and are rarely used outside of school. Indeed, it may be that the current emphasis on learning disability in American schools is primarily a reflection of a technologically complex society's concern about literacy.

**How is ability/disability evident in your life?**

_____

_____

_____

_____

## *Social Class*

Social class is culturally defined on the basis of those criteria on which a person or social group may be ranked in relation to others in a stratified (or layered) society. There is considerable debate about the criteria that determine social class. Some identify class membership primarily in terms of wealth and its origin (inherited or newly earned). Other commonly used criteria include the amount of one's education, power, and influence.

**How is social class evident in your life?**

_____

_____

_____

_____

## *Ethnicity/Nationality*

Ethnicity is culturally defined according to the knowledge, beliefs, and behavior patterns shared by a group of people with the same history and the same language. Ethnicity carries a strong sense of "peoplehood," that is, of loyalty to a "community of memory" (Bellah, Madsen, Sullivan, Swindler, and Tipton, 1985). It is also related to the ecological niche in which an ethnic group has found itself and to adaptations people make to those environmental conditions.

The category of nationality is culturally defined on the basis of shared citizenship that may or may not include a shared ethnicity. In the contemporary world, the population of most nations includes citizens (and resident noncitizens) who vary in ethnicity. While we are accustomed to this idea in the United States, we are sometimes unaware that it is also the case in other nations. Thus, we tend to identify all people from Japan as Japanese, all people from France as French, and so forth. Similarly, when American citizens of varying ethnic identities go abroad, they tend to be identified as "Americans." Being Chinese-American, for instance, may mean little outside the borders of the United States.

**How are the concepts of ethnicity and nationality evident in your life?**

_____

_____

_____

_____

### Religion/Spirituality

Religion and spirituality are culturally defined on the basis of a shared set of ideas about the relationship of the earth and the people on it to a deity or deities and a shared set of rules for living moral values that will enhance that relationship. A set of behaviors identified with worship is also commonly shared. Religious identity may include membership in a worldwide-organized religion (e.g., Islam, Christianity, Judaism, Buddhism, Taoism), or in smaller (but also worldwide) sects belonging to each of the larger religions (e.g., Catholic or Protestant Christianity, or Conservative, Reformed, or Hasidic Judaism). Religious identity may also include a large variety of spiritualistic religions, sometimes called pagan or Goddess religions. These are often but not always associated with indigenous peoples in the Americas and other parts of the world.

**How are religion and/or spirituality evident in your life?**

_____

_____

_____

_____

### Geographic Location

Geographic location is culturally defined by the characteristics (topographical features, natural resources) of the ecological environment in which one lives. This may include the characteristics of one's neighborhood or community (rural, suburban, urban), and/or the natural and climatic features of one's region (mountainous, desert, plains, coastal, hot, cold, wet, dry). It has been argued that in the United States, one's regional identity functions in the same way as one's national heritage. Thus southerners, westerners, and midwesterners are identified and often identify themselves as members of ethniclike groups, with the same kinds of loyalties, sense of community, and language traits.

**How is geographic or regional identity evident in your life?**

_____

_____

_____

_____

### Age

Age is culturally defined according to the length of time one has lived and the state of physical and mental development one has attained. Chronological age is measured in different ways by different social groups or societies. Some calculate it in calendar years, others by natural cycles such as phases of the moon, and still others by the marking of major natural or social events. Most humans view such development as a matter of "stages," but the nature and particular characteristics of each "stage" may differ widely. In most western societies, for example, age cohort groups are usually identified as infancy, childhood, adolescence, adulthood, and old age. "Normal" development markers include the acquisition of motor and language skills (infancy and childhood), the ability to understand and use abstract concepts (childhood and adolescence), and the ability to assume responsibility for oneself and others (adolescence and adulthood). In other societies, these cohort groups may differ. For example, in many nonwestern societies, the cohort group we define as adolescents may not exist at all, and the classifications of childhood and old age may be longer or shorter. Also, different societies place different value on age, some placing more emphasis on youth while others venerate the aged.

**How is age evident in your life?**

_____

_____

_____

_____

### Sexuality

Sexuality is culturally defined on the basis of particular patterns of sexual self-identification, behavior, and interpersonal relationships (Herek, 1986). There is growing evidence that one's sexual orientation is, in part, a function of one's innate biological characteristics (LeVay and Hunter, 1994). Culturally speaking, sexuality is tied to a number of factors: sexual behavior, gender identity (both internal and external), affiliation, and role behavior. Like health, sexuality has a variety of orientations. Because sexuality is frequently linked to one's deepest, most meaningful experiences (both religious and interpersonal), people who deviate from socially approved norms are often socially ostracized and sometimes physically abused or even killed. This is currently the case with homosexuality in the United States, where the prevailing view of sexuality is bimodal; only male and female are identified as possibilities. In other societies, additional possibilities are available. The Lakota Sioux, for example, approve four sexual orientations: biological males who possess largely masculine traits, biological males who possess largely feminine traits, biological females who possess largely feminine traits, and biological females who possess largely masculine traits. The role of the female-identified male in Lakota society is called _berdache,_ and is accorded high honor as possessing multiple traits and characteristics. _Berdache_ tend to be teachers and artists, and if a _berdache_ takes an interest in one's child or children, it is considered to be an advantage.

**How is sexuality evident in your life?**

_____

_____

_____

_____

## Language

The cultural definition of language is "a shared system of vocal sounds and/or non-verbal behaviors by which members of a group communicate with one another" (Gollnick and Chinn, 1990). Language may be the most significant source of cultural learning because it is through language that most other cultural knowledge is acquired. Considerable research on the relation of brain function to language gives evidence that human beings are "hard wired" for language development at a particular stage in brain development (Chomsky, 1966). That is, children who are in the company of other people appear to be "programmed" to learn whatever spoken language or sign system is used around them. Children even invent their own language systems, complete with syntactical structures, if no other language is available. It may also be that this "program" decreases in power (or disappears altogether) at a certain point, helping to explain why it is more difficult for older children and adults to acquire a new language. Language is meaningful in terms of both its verbal properties (what we "name" things, people, ideas), and in terms of its nonverbal properties (its norms regarding interpersonal distance, meaningful gestures, and so forth).

**How is language evident in your life?**

_____

_____

_____

_____

## Social Status

Social status is culturally defined on the basis of the prestige, social esteem, and/or honor accorded an individual or group by other social groups or by society (Berger and Berger, 1972). Social status cuts across the other categories, since every social group or society appears to construct hierarchies of honor, prestige, and value with which to "sort out" its members, often on the basis of such attributes as race, age, gender, ability, religion, and so forth. In some cases, social status varies with social class; in many other cases, however, social class does not explain one's status in a social group or society. Thus, persons may occupy a high place in the class system in terms of income and power but not be accorded prestige or honor. The children of a newly wealthy family who can well afford to be sent to Harvard, for example, may have little prestige among the sons and daughters of inherited wealth. Similarly, there may be people accorded high status in the society who occupy relatively low-class positions. In U.S. society, many entertainers and sports figures fit this description.

**How is social status evident in your life?**

_____

_____

_____

_____

While there is some overlap among these twelve attributes of culture, the important point to remember is that a particular society or social group culturally defines each of them. The cultural identity of all individuals (i.e., their knowledge, attitudes, values, and skills) is formed through one's experience with these twelve attributes.

Now, look closely at the twelve attributes of culture listed below. Allow these to represent some of the hundreds of cultural influences that impact each individual, including yourself. Take the time to examine your own background in terms of each of these. While before you merely identified how each of these attributes was evident in your life, _here you should examine how your views on the world, your behavior, and your values have been influenced by each of these._

For instance, for geographic location, a student might say she or he is from the state of Washington, which is relatively conservative but quite environmentally responsible. The person might value the wilderness and nature in general, and enjoy being outdoors.

**Race:**

_____

_____

_____

_____

**Sex/gender:**

_____

_____

_____

_____

**Health:**

_____

_____

_____

_____

**Ability/disability:**

_____

_____

_____

_____

**Social Class:**

_____

_____

_____

_____

**Ethnicity/nationality:**

_____

_____

_____

_____

**Religion/spirituality:**

_____

_____

_____

_____

**Geographic location:**

_____

_____

_____

_____

**Age:**

_____

_____

_____

_____

**Sexuality:**

_____

_____

_____

_____

**Language:**

_____

_____

_____

_____

**Social status:**

_____

_____

_____

_____

**Which of the attributes holds the most significance for you?**

_____

_____

_____

_____

_____

_____

_____

**Which of the attributes holds the least significance for you?**

_____

_____

_____

_____

**How is involvement in the groups that are important to you expressed in your day-to-day life?**

_____

_____

_____

_____

**Give examples of experiences you have had that have increased or decreased your sense of belonging to a certain group.**

_____

_____

_____

_____

**Which groups place you at an advantage in American society? How?**

_____

_____

_____

_____

_____

_____

_____

**Which groups place you at a disadvantage in American society? How?**

_____

_____

_____

_____

_____

_____

_____

**Share your responses with others in small groups. Were there some aspects that were more difficult to discuss than others? What do you notice about the different responses provided by peers who you consider to be in a similar group as you? What does this suggest about within-group differences?**

_____

_____

_____

_____

_____

_____

_____

part two

# Getting to Know the Culture of Others: Intercultural Interaction

## Activity 11

# Adjustment to Change

## Purpose

To identify the emotional responses that can occur during a major transition experience, and relate them to international and/or intercultural adjustment.

## Instructions

What major transitions have you had in your life? Identify one that extended over a rather lengthy period of time. Perhaps you moved to another state, another section of town, or a new neighborhood within your town or city. Perhaps you recall beginning a new school, going to summer camp, or moving into a dormitory as a freshman in college. Draw a graph in the space on the next page that traces your emotional responses during that experience from the time when you first began the experience until the time when you felt completely "at home."

## *My Transition Experience*

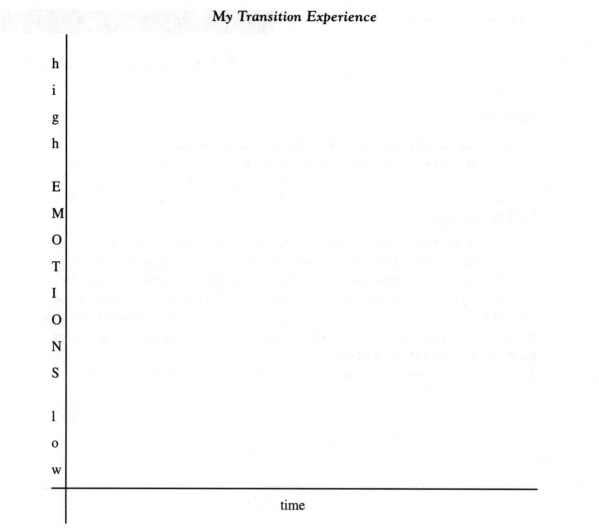

Cross-cultural trainers consider adjustment to be an on-going process that is experienced in five general phases: pre-departure or pre-contact, arrival or initial meetings, culture shock, culture learning where relationships are built, and pre-departure and re-entry. What phases of your experience reflect ones that are similar to the adjustment process?

_____

_____

_____

_____

_____

To what do you attribute major changes in your graph? What helped you overcome any difficulties you may have encountered?

_____

_____

_____

_____

_____

What would you suggest to others as they encounter similar major adjustments in their lives?

_____

_____

_____

_____

_____

How might you use your experience to prepare for a significant cross-cultural encounter?

_____

_____

_____

_____

How might the adjustment process be evident for students in schools? For teachers?
For parents?

**For students:**

_____

_____

_____

_____

_____

**For teachers:**

_____

_____

_____

_____

_____

**For parents:**

_____

_____

_____

_____

_____

# A Culture-General Framework for Understanding Intercultural Interactions

## Purpose

To identify concepts that cut across diversity and have an impact on intercultural interactions in the school, classroom, and community.

## Instructions

Read the following content and respond to the reflective questions that follow.

It is rather difficult to think about preparing people to interact with others of any specific culture given the diversity of most schools and communities in the United States. Fortunately, researchers in the fields of cross-cultural psychology and intercultural training have identified concepts and experiences people are certain to confront regardless of their own background, the cultures with which they are interacting, and their particular role in the new cultural setting. One useful model, presented by Cushner and Brislin (1996), is referred to as the *18-Theme Culture-General Framework*. Because this model is deliberately general, its usefulness lies in its adaptability to any intercultural encounter. This model allows us to capture the experience of cultural differences from a variety of perspectives (emotional, informational, and developmental), and to offer frameworks within which specific problem situations can be addressed.

## Stage One: Understanding Emotional Responses in Intercultural Interaction

In any intercultural encounter, people's emotions are quickly aroused when they meet with unpredictable behavior on the part of others or when their own behavior does not bring about anticipated responses. It is important to note that the nature and strength of these emotional reactions quite often surprise the people involved. This is often the case with students from some backgrounds who may not have anticipated the differences between their own culture and that of the school. It is also the case for teachers who find themselves in a school or classroom context that is significantly different from their prior experience. Recognizing, understanding, and accommodating the strong emotional responses people are certain to have when involved in intercultural interactions is critical to successfully negotiating them. Below is a list of the emotional responses people most often confront when interacting with an unfamiliar culture. A brief discussion of these responses follows.

*Anxiety*
*Ambiguity*
*Disconfirmed Expectations*
*Belonging/Rejection*
*Confronting Personal Prejudice*

**Anxiety:** As individuals encounter unexpected or unfamiliar behavior of others, they are likely to become anxious about whether or not their own behavior is appropriate. Children in new schools, families in new communities, and teachers in new schools will all experience some degree of anxiety as they attempt to modify their own behavior to fit the new circumstances. Feelings of anxiety may result in a strong desire to avoid a situation altogether, and individuals sometimes go to great lengths to do so, all the while rationalizing their avoidance behavior on other grounds.

Can you think of times when **anxiety** was evident in your life and how it might have interfered with your ability to function most effectively?

_____

_____

_____

_____

_____

**Ambiguity:** When interacting with those who are culturally different, the messages received from the other person are often unclear, yet decisions must be made and appropriate behavior somehow produced. Most people, when faced with an ambiguous situation, try to resolve it by applying culturally familiar criteria. People who are effective at working across cultures are known to have a high tolerance for ambiguity. That is, in situations where they do not have full understanding of what is going on, they are skilled at asking appropriate questions and modifying their behavior accordingly.

Can you recall times when things have been **ambiguous**, unclear, or uncomfortable for you, yet you still had to function? What did you do that helped you to do what needed to be done?

_____

_____

_____

_____

_____

**Disconfirmed Expectations:** Individuals may become upset or uncomfortable, not because of the specific circumstances they encounter but because the situation differs from what they expect. Despite our recognition that differences are all around us, we have a tendency to expect others to think and behave in ways similar to ourselves. Most people interact with others expecting that others will think and behave according to preconceived, often inaccurate notions. They then act on those inaccurate judgments, and find that their actions do not produce the intended result.

Can you recall a time when you experienced **disconfirmed expectations** and thought the situation would be one way when in fact it was quite different? How did you reconcile this difference?

_____

_____

_____

_____

_____

**Belonging/Rejection:** People have a need to fill a social niche, to feel that they "belong" and are "at home" in the social milieu in which they find themselves. When people are immersed in an intercultural interaction this sense of belonging may be difficult to achieve because they may not know the "rules" of behavior in the new situation. Rather, they often feel rejected as an "outsider." When this sense of rejection is strong enough they may become alienated from the situation altogether. Students, for example, who may feel alienated from the classroom or school are more likely to become discipline problems and have difficulty paying attention to classroom work.

Can you recall a time when you felt as if you did not **belong**? How did this make you feel? How did you respond? What might you suggest to another who has similar feelings?

---

---

---

---

**Confronting Personal Prejudice:** Finally, when involved in cross-cultural interactions, one may be forced to acknowledge that previously held beliefs about a certain group of people or certain kinds of behaviors may be inaccurate or without foundation. Such a revelation may result in embarrassment or shame. It may also require a basic change in one's attitude and behavior toward others. And, since change is difficult even in the best of circumstances, people often continue to harbor their prejudices even when faced with contradictory evidence.

Can you think of a **prejudice** you might harbor about certain people? Can you think of times when you found that your information about certain people was not accurate or true?

---

---

---

---

---

## Stage Two: Understanding the Cultural Basis of Unfamiliar Behavior

In addition to accommodating their feelings, both parties in an intercultural encounter need to understand the cultural influences that direct one another's knowledge base as a means of understanding one another's behavior. Individuals typically try to understand another person's behavior according to their own cultural patterns. Put another way, since most people do not have extensive experiences with people who think and act differently from themselves, they tend to interpret another's behavior in terms of their own cultural frame of reference. In brief, we see what we expect to see, and with incomplete information or inaccurate knowledge, we may make inappropriate judgments about a given situation.

A relatively common example may illustrate this point. Some children from certain cultural groups (e.g., some, but certainly not all, Latino and African American children) are taught to demonstrate respect for elders or persons in authority by avoiding eye contact. Hence a child being reprimanded by a parent or teacher may avoid gazing in that person's eyes. On the other hand, most European American children (who end up being the majority of the teachers in schools) are taught to look a person of authority directly in the eye. Imagine the outcome of an interaction involving an African American or Latino child being reprimanded by a European American teacher. The child, as she or he has been taught, may look away from the gaze of the teacher to demonstrate respect. The teacher, expecting eye contact as a sign of respect, interprets the child's behavior as suggesting that "He or she is not listening to me," or "This child does not respect me." This incorrect judgment may jeopardize future interactions between this particular teacher, student, and family.

The individual skilled in intercultural encounters learns to seek alternative explanations of unexpected behavior rather than simply interpreting such behavior according to his or her own cultural framework. The question, "Why is this behavior occurring?" precedes the question, "What is the matter with this child?"

There are many components of cultural knowledge, each of which reaches the individual through a network of socializing agents. Regardless of the complexity of this socialization process, the resulting knowledge base functions to give us satisfactory explanations of the world, and tells us how best to interact with other people. Within this knowledge base, however, the following kinds of knowledge are likely to differ across cultures.

*Communication and Language Use*
*Values*
*Rituals and Superstition*
*Situational Behavior*
*Roles*
*Social Status*
*Time and Space*
*The Group versus the Individual*

**Communication and Language Use.** Communication differences are probably the most obvious problem to be overcome when crossing cultural boundaries. This is the case whether the **languages** involved are completely different (e.g., Japanese, Kiswahili, English, American Sign Language), are similar in root but not in evolution (e.g., French, Italian, Spanish), or are variations or dialects of the same language (e.g., French and French-Canadian, English and Ebonics). In any case, many people find it difficult to learn a second (or third) language. In addition, **nonverbal communication**

customs such as facial expressions, gestures, and so forth, differ across cultures so that what a particular gesture means to one person may have a very different meaning to someone from another culture.

Can you think of instances where you have encountered **communication differences**, both verbal as well as nonverbal?

_____

_____

_____

_____

**Values:** The development of internalized values is one of the chief socialization goals in all societies. Values provide social cohesion among group members and are often codified into laws or rules for living, such as the Ten Commandments for Christians and Jews or the Hippocratic Oath for doctors. The range of possible values with respect to any particular issue is usually wide, deeply held, and often difficult to change. For example, in the dominant culture of the United States, belief in "progress" is highly valued and almost religious in character. A teacher subscribing to that value may have a very difficult time interacting with the parents of a young woman who seems not to value her academic potential. The young woman's parents may believe that she should assume the traditional role of wife and mother after high school rather than seek a college education. The teacher, on the other hand, may believe that the young woman should "look to the future," "change with the times," and "make progress" for herself. These are not small differences.

Can you recall instances where **value differences** came between you and someone else? How did you reconcile these differences?

_____

_____

_____

_____

_____

**Ritual and Superstitions:** All social groups develop **rituals** that help members meet the demands of everyday life. Such rituals vary in significance from rubbing a rabbit's foot before a stressful event to the intricate format of an organized religious service. The difficulty, however, is that the rituals of one culture may be viewed as **superstitions** by members of other cultures. Increasingly, children from a wide variety of religious and cultural backgrounds bring to school behaviors that are often misunderstood and labeled "superstitious" by others in the school or community.

Can you think of instances where one person's **rituals** may be interpreted by others to be **superstitious?** Can you provide an example that might be evident in the school context?

_____

_____

_____

_____

_____

**Situational Behavior:** Knowing how to behave appropriately in a variety of settings and situations is important to all people. The "rules" for behavior in a particular context are internalized at an early age and can be easily perceived to be "broken" by one who has internalized a different set of rules for the same setting or situation. Examples of this can be found in the workplace, in social settings, in schools, when making decisions and solving problems, and deciding whom one should turn to in time of need.

Can you think of instances where the rules and behavior you thought were appropriate to follow were not expected in a certain context? How did you react? What did you do to resolve the difference?

_____

_____

_____

_____

**Role:** Knowledge of appropriate **role behavior**, like that of situational behavior, may vary from situation to situation and from group to group. How one behaves as a mother or father, for example, may be different from how one behaves as a teacher. Likewise, gender- and age-related behavior between groups may also differ in a significant manner.

Can you think of examples of how certain **role-based behavior** might differ across cultures?

_____

_____

_____

_____

**Social Status:** All social groups make distinctions based on markers of high and low status. **Social class** and **social status** are both the results of stratification systems, whose role assignments may vary considerably from group to group. The role of "aunt" in the African American community, for example, may hold much higher status than it does in middle-class, European American society, with the aunt of an African American child bearing a considerable responsibility for the well-being of that child. Middle-class European American teachers, when confronted by a very proactive aunt and unaware of this status and relationship, may believe that the child's mother is somehow shirking her duties.

Can you think of instances where you might have misinterpreted a given person's status? What kinds of problems might this have caused?

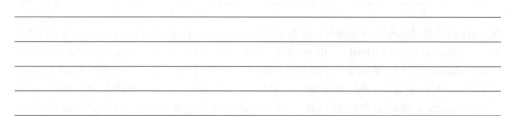

**Time and Space:** Differences in conceptions of time and space may also vary among social groups. In addition to differences in the divisions of time (e.g., a week, a crop harvest), groups vary in the degree to which time is valued. It is common for European Americans, for example, to value punctuality since that is seen as an expression of respect. However, measures of time and their value may be much more elastic in less-industrialized societies where work is less synchronized. Similarly, the ease and comfort of one's position in space vis-a-vis other people may vary. How close one stands to another when speaking, and the degree to which one should stand face-to-face with another, are both subject to cultural variation.

Can you recall instances where your concept of **time** differed in a significant way from another person? Can you think of instances when another's use of **space** seemed to interfere with yours?

_____

_____

_____

_____

_____

**Relationship to the Group versus the Individual:** All people sometimes act according to their **individual interests** and sometimes according to their **group allegiances**. The relative emphasis on group versus individual orientation varies from group to group and may significantly affect the choices one makes. People from more collective societies, for instance, may defer decisionmaking to other elders or relatives. People from more individualistic societies, on the other hand, may be socialized to make most decisions pretty much on their own.

Can you think of instances when people were responding more to the **collective** or **group** when you would have done otherwise? Or when people stood more on their own when you would have expected them to look to others for guidance and support?

_____

_____

_____

_____

_____

## Stage Three: Making Adjustments and Reshaping Cultural Identity

Finally, as a result of prolonged intercultural interactions, an individual may experience profound personal change. That is, an individual's way of perceiving the world, processing those perceptions, and viewing themselves as well as others may alter. Typically, for example, individuals who have had significant intercultural experiences become more complex thinkers. This is, of course, one of the central goals of multicultural education since it enables people to handle more culturally complex stimuli, to be accurate in their interpretations of others' behavior, and thus to deal more effectively with the differences they encounter. As individuals continue to have intercultural experiences, they become less culture-bound and more understanding of how others perceive the world. Such individuals can now "see" from another point of view; they are more complex thinkers and can handle a greater variety of diverse information. They are also less likely to make inaccurate judgments or attributions because they have the ability to inquire into behavior and beliefs they do not comprehend, thereby improving their understanding. Think back to the gaze-avoidance behavior in the interaction between the European American teacher and the Latino or African American child referred to earlier. The interculturally knowledgeable teacher would understand the meaning behind the child's gaze-avoidance and thus more accurately judge the child to be listening and demonstrating respect.

While a person may have limited knowledge of the content of other cultures, we do know that all people *process information* in similar ways. Important ways of processing information are listed below, each of which can be investigated by the participants in intercultural exchanges.

> *Categorization*
> *Differentiation*
> *Attribution*
> *Ingroups—Outgroups*
> *Learning Style*

**Categorization:** Since people cannot attend to all the information presented to them, they create **categories** for organizing and responding to similar bits of information. Cultural stereotypes, for example, are categories usually associated with particular groups of people. People involved in intercultural interactions often categorize one another quickly according to whatever category systems they have learned.

Can you think of situations where miscategorization was evident, that is, when one person or group of people **categorized** certain information in one manner while another individual or group **categorized** it differently?

_____

_____

_____

_____

_____

**Differentiation:** Information related to highly meaningful categories becomes more highly refined or **differentiated**. As a result, new categories may be formed. Such refinement or differentiation is usually shared only among people who have had many experiences in common (e.g., doctors) and thus may be unknown even to those whose general background is similar. A good example of this process is the way in which people in Asia might differentiate the food "rice." Because it is an extremely important part of their diet, and thus way of life, it can be referred to in many different ways, by many different terms, and can have many different uses. For most European Americans, rice is not as important and, thus, fewer references are made to it. Or consider students in a particular high school who differentiate their peers into groups such as "brains," "nerds," and "jocks." While a similar type of differentiation may occur in most high schools, the particular categories and their meaning may differ considerably from school to school.

Can you think of other elements in your culture that are highly **differentiated** but may not be so highly differentiated by others? Or, can you think of examples of an element from another culture that is highly differentiated but is not so important in your own group?

_____

_____

_____

_____

**Attribution:** People not only perceive others according to familiar categories, they also make judgments about others based on the behavior they observe. People judge others, for example, as competent or incompetent, educated or naive, well-intentioned or ill-intentioned. Psychologists call these judgments **attributions**, and tell us that within about seven seconds of meeting someone new, initial judgments are made. These initial 'sizing-up' judgments, once made, are usually quite resistant to change. Human judgments, however, are fallible, and certain errors occur repeatedly in human thought. One of these, called the **fundamental attribution error**, describes the tendency people have to judge others on different sets of criteria than they apply to themselves. Thus, if a person fails at a given task, he or she is more likely to look to the situation for an explanation: it was too hot, someone else was unfair to the person, the task was unreasonable. If a person observes someone else fail at a task, he or she is more likely to explain the failure in terms of the other person's traits: she is lazy, he is uneducated, she is uncaring. This tendency is even more prevalent in cross-cultural situations because there is so much behavior that is unfamiliar. Given the speed with which people make judgments and the probable lack of intercultural understanding, attribution errors abound in intercultural situations.

Can you provide examples when you may have judged a situation differently from someone else? Or, can you think of a time when someone made an inaccurate attribution about you that differed from how you would have judged yourself?

_____

_____

_____

_____

_____

_____

**In-groups and Out-groups:** People the world over divide others into groups with which they are comfortable and can discuss their concerns (**in-groups**) and those who are kept at a distance (**out-groups**), oftentimes based on their own system of categorization and differentiation. Those entering new cultural situations must recognize that they will often be considered members of the out-group and will not share certain in-group behavior and communication, at least at the outset. As a result, people may be kept from participating in certain in-group activities, such as may happen when work-mates get together on Friday after a week of work.

Can you think of a situation where you thought you would be included in the in-group but were not, or when you got together with your in-group and others were left out? Can you think of times when others might be excluded for no other reason than they were not considered a part of a particular in-group?

_____

_____

_____

_____

_____

**Learning style:** Sometimes called cognitive style, learning style refers to one's preferred method of learning and is very much under cultures' influence. How (and what) one perceives, the categories into which one places sensory stimuli, and whether learning is preferred through observation, listening, or action are all, in part, culturally based. Learning styles are partly the result of strengths and weaknesses in sensory perception (one's hearing may be more acute than one's vision, for example). However, it is also the case that cultural patterning may teach a child to attend to certain kinds of stimuli rather than others, as when children from collectivist societies learn better in cooperative groups.

Can you think of culturally based examples of where one's **learning style** might be in conflict with the teaching style of the teacher?

_____

_____

_____

_____

_____

_____

# Critical Incident Review

## Purpose

To apply the 18-theme culture-general framework to critical incidents in an educational context.

## Instructions

Imagine what might happen in any intercultural interchange. People have certain expectations of the outcomes of their own behavior as well as the motivations of others. Add to this the fact that people have a tendency to make judgments or attributions about others based on the behavior they observe. Such expectations come primarily from their own socialization, predisposing them to view the world from one particular perspective. When people's expectations are not met, they must reconcile the difference between the reality and their expectations (**disconfirmed expectations**). Such is the basis of the strong emotional reaction in cultural conflict. Many outcomes are possible, including:

> People may feel extremely emotional and get upset, oftentimes without knowing what is at play as culture is often a secret. As such, they may have a tendency to avoid further cross-cultural encounters because they are perceived as unpleasant;

and/or

> People may make **faulty attributions**, or assign inaccurate interpretations to the meaning and intentions of someone's behavior, accusing her or him of lacking sufficient knowledge, cheating, being pushy — in other words, interpreting events from their own ethnocentric perspective and thus judging others by inappropriate standards;

and/or

> People may begin to inquire about how others interpret or find meaning in their world. As people begin to learn how others understand and operate from their own perspective or subjective culture, true culture learning begins to take place. This suggests that people have a need to broaden their knowledge base about others and about their own socialization as well as that of others.

The culture-general framework provides one such foundation of knowledge concerning issues at play in intercultural interaction. Building such a knowledge base enables individuals to understand and overcome the oftentimes unexpected but strong emotions they are certain to encounter in themselves; to be more precise and accurate in their interpretations of others' behavior; and thus, to interact more effectively with those different from themselves.

Following are a number of critical incidents designed to help you develop a foundation in the culture-general framework. Read each incident, respond to the questions that immediately follow, and select the alternative that best explains the situation. Feedback on your responses is provided at the end of this activity.

An alternative strategy for working with critical incidents is to do the following in small groups:

1. Read and discuss one incident. Be certain everyone understands the situation.
2. Rank order the alternative explanations. Which can you agree are probably the most insightful explanations?
3. Then read the rationales that provide feedback on your choices.
4. Identify which of the 18 culture-general themes you think help explain the situation.
5. Relate the theme(s) to your own experience and/or to an educational setting. How have you observed this theme in action? How do you think it might be present in various classroom settings?

## A Model Minority

Wellington Chang was a sixth-grade student in a San Francisco neighborhood elementary school. Recently arrived from Hong Kong, he spoke very functional, though accented, English.

His sixth-grade class was multiethnic with students of African American, Latino, and various Asian backgrounds, as well as a few European Americans. His teacher, Mr. Fenwick, was a competent teacher with more than 25 years' experience in the classroom. Of German heritage, Mr. Fenwick had watched as the district's population was transformed into an incredibly heterogeneous mixture of ethnic and linguistic groups. He prided himself on his ability to adapt to the ever-changing and complex environment.

Though Wellington seemed quiet enough at first, he increasingly exhibited what Mr. Fenwick described as disruptive behavior, including talking, laughing, and teasing other students. This perplexed Mr. Fenwick since his experience with Chinese young people was that they were among the most hard-working and diligent students. Far from being disruptive, Mr. Fenwick found most Chinese students to be relatively passive individuals whom he had to encourage to be more participatory. Thus Wellington's behavior seemed to him particularly disturbing and he punished him more severely than other non-Chinese students, even though his behavior was no worse than theirs. The principal noticed this discrepancy and brought it to Mr. Fenwick's attention.

If you were the principal, how would you address this with Mr. Fenwick? From the 18-theme culture-general framework, what issues might be operating unconsciously to explain Mr. Fenwick's behavior?

_____

_____

_____

_____

_____

_____

_____

_____

Now, given the following alternatives, which provides the most insight into the situation?

1. Mr. Fenwick believes that no matter where they come from, all Chinese will behave in the same manner.
2. Mr. Fenwick is operating from very limited experience with ethnic minorities in the United States and does not realize that Wellington's behavior is well within the normal range for U.S. sixth-graders, regardless of their background.
3. Mr. Fenwick's expectations about the Chinese being a model minority cause him to judge Wellington too harshly.
4. For some reason, Mr. Fenwick has taken a personal dislike to Wellington.

Feedback on these alternatives can be found on page 87.

## Typical American Practice

"Class, I'd like you to welcome Keiko, an exchange student from Japan, who will be attending Central High School for the second semester," said Mr. Cooper at the beginning of his American Government class. Keiko had experienced similar introductions in all of her classes during her first day of school in the United States. The friendliness of the faculty and students impressed her and made her feel right at home.

As time went on, however, Keiko felt that the teachers and students were ignoring her more and more. Very few students talked to her, and only a couple offered a brief greeting in the hallway or cafeteria. Some students, and even families, after talking with her for a while, left saying things like, "We'll have to get together some time," or "I'll call you soon." This rarely seemed to happen, however. And although Keiko received mostly As in class, her teachers hardly ever called on her in class. She began to wonder if she had somehow offended the people at her new school, and she gradually became withdrawn and isolated.

What do you think has happened here to cause this unfortunate situation? From the 18-theme culture-general framework, what issues might be operating to explain the situation?

_____

_____

_____

_____

_____

_____

_____

_____

_____

_____

_____

_____

_____

Given the following alternatives, which would you select as most appropriate?

1. The students resent Keiko's high grades and are showing their jealousy of her.
2. Americans have a tendency to offer foreigners a special welcome and then quickly treat them like everyone else.
3. Keiko demands too much attention and has unrealistic expectations that everyone will treat her in a special way.
4. The faculty members are obviously insincere in their initial welcomes. They are probably acting on a directive from the principal.

Feedback on these alternatives can be found on page 88.

## The Students Are Anxious, but Why?

It was test week throughout the city, and teachers and parents were anxious about how things would go this time around. In previous years the district's scores were among the lowest in the state, and the school had been placed on Academic Emergency.

Today Mary McConnell was exhausted! Normally she could cope with the challenges of being homeroom teacher for ninth graders, but today had been extremely difficult. All morning her students had taken standardized tests and they had been "impossible." They had taken a long time to settle down in their seats; everyone had to sharpen their two required pencils, and halfway through the process, the pencil sharpener had mysteriously broken.

One boy just would not stop talking and cracking jokes from the back of the room. He was often encouraged by remarks and giggles from the girls around him. Two girls had flatly refused to take the tests, and Ms. McConnell had sent them to the principal's office. Three students had marked their answer sheets in patterns without even reading the questions. Ms. McConnell had tried to enlist the students' genuine participation, but they had refused. Two of them then put their heads down on their desks and would not respond to her at all.

Mary McConnell knew she was facing a high level of resistance in the room; however, she could not understand what was going on. Can you? What would you recommend she do? From the 18-theme culture-general framework, what issues might be operating to explain the circumstances?

_____

_____

_____

_____

_____

_____

_____

_____

_____

_____

_____

_____

_____

Of the four alternatives below, select the response that, to you, best explains the situation.

1. The students were very anxious because they didn't like the strict time limits of standardized tests.
2. These students had scored low on standardized tests in previous years and, because they expected to do so again, felt quite anxious.
3. When the pencil sharpener broke and the students couldn't sharpen their pencils, they became anxious about marking their answer sheets correctly.
4. The students did not like their daily classroom routine interrupted by such a long activity.

Feedback on these alternatives can be found on page 88.

# The Art Awards Ceremony

Tony, an African American high school student, had an interest in art that he pursued on his own by visiting museums, reading books, sketching, and painting. Much of his work reflected his African American heritage. Tony enrolled at midterm in the predominantly white JFK High School. He took an art class and was encouraged by his teacher to develop his talent. Tony entered several paintings in the school art show, received praise and attention for his work, and went on to enter the all-city show, where he also did well. The longtime principal of his school, a middle-aged European American, Mr. Tarbell, was present at the awards ceremony and was delighted that one of his students received rave reviews and an award. Congratulating Tony he said, "Good work, Tony. We are proud to have such a talented black student representing our school. You have an uncanny ability to paint."

Mr. Tarbell was surprised when Tony simply walked away from him with no comment.

What do you think is going on in this incident? From the 18-theme culture-general framework, what issues might help to explain Tony's behavior?

_____

_____

_____

_____

_____

_____

_____

_____

Of the following explanations, how might this behavior best be interpreted?

1. Tony was overwhelmed by all the attention and uncomfortable around someone in Mr. Tarbell's position.
2. Tony was offended by what Mr. Tarbell said.
3. Tony's friends likely motioned for him to come join them. Caught up in the excitement, he simply went on over to them.
4. Tony, embarrassed and not used to the praise he was receiving, especially from the school administration, left feeling uncomfortable.

Feedback on these alternatives can be found on page 89.

## The Missed Meeting

Mrs. Conant, an 11th grade social studies teacher, was concerned that a newly arrived Lebanese student, Rema, was having difficulty in dealing with the material in her U.S. History textbook. After Rema failed two consecutive tests, Mrs. Conant called Rema's parents and arranged a conference for 9:45 a.m. on Thursday during her free period.

Before school on Thursday, Mrs. Conant prepared a list of her questions, concerns, and recommendations regarding Rema and was looking forward to meeting the parents. After teaching her first class, she made certain that the central office secretary would direct the couple to her room, and then she returned there at 9:30 to await their arrival. As 9:45 and then 10:00 passed and no one showed, Mrs. Conant became increasingly puzzled and irritated.

When the clock read 10:10, Mrs. Conant assumed the parents had forgotten about the appointment or had experienced car trouble. Therefore, she decided to spend the remainder of her free period in the faculty lounge. On her way out the door, however, she met the parents, who introduced themselves and said how happy they were to have the opportunity to discuss their daughter's progress. They made no mention of their lateness and offered no apology or explanation.

Mrs. Conant, trying to hide her anger, told them that she had only a few minutes left and tersely explained her perceptions of Rema's difficulties. When the parents began to give some feedback, the bell rang for the next class. Mrs. Conant cut them off, explaining that she had another class to teach. The parents, looking confused and insulted, left an angry Mrs. Conant returning to teach her class.

What would you say is the best explanation of the underlying problem of this unfortunate incident?

Now, of the following alternative explanations, which do you think best explains the cultural difference that may be operating?

1. Mrs. Conant was overly concerned about Rema's minor academic problems. A conference was really unnecessary, and the parents felt resentful about being summoned to school and didn't really want to come in the first place.

2. The parents were obviously at fault for being so late. Their lack of consideration for a teacher's valuable time indicates they are just not very concerned about their daughter or the feelings of others.

3. The parents and Mrs. Conant differ in their outlook on time and punctuality. Being 20 to 25 minutes late was no big deal to the parents, but it was very important to the teacher.

4. Mrs. Conant resents having to give up her free period to have parent-teacher conferences.

Feedback on these alternatives can be found on page 90.

## Careful Preparation of Lectures

Robert, an experienced agricultural engineering professor from New England, felt extremely fortunate to have been invited to spend four weeks in Texas training four groups of young, English-speaking immigrant Mexican American farm workers. Each week he was to teach a different group in the use and maintenance of some new farm machinery that they were excited about using.

Robert spent hours in the instructional lab constructing diagrams explaining the use of the machines as well as maintenance of their parts. He was especially pleased with the diagrams he made that explained possible problems and actions one should take when a problem occurred. This media, combined with his extensive lecture notes, company operating manuals, videos, books, and computer software would assure the success of the program.

Much to his surprise, Robert found this teaching experience to be an extreme struggle both for himself and for his students. The first day seemed to go well, but the remaining four seemed long and drawn out. The students often complained about a lack of understanding. They were restless, talkative, and seemingly uninterested in what Robert had to offer. This really confused Robert as he had assumed that the students would be eager to learn the use of these machines that would ultimately improve crop yield.

What do you think is the source of the problem here?

_____

_____

_____

_____

_____

_____

_____

_____

Of the following, which best explains the situation?

1. Robert's students were much younger than those he had initially been trained to teach.
2. Robert ignored the fact that most of his students speak Spanish (most commonly, Tex-Mex) as well as English. He should have incorporated this into his presentation.
3. Migrant Mexican-American farm workers are not accustomed to learning from books and papers. They often prefer to be taught with the real object.
4. The students resented Robert pushing his new technology on them and did not want this new machinery interfering with the methods to which they were accustomed.

Feedback on these alternatives can be found on page 90.

## The Chemistry Lab

Miguel, a 16-year-old Mexican student in Denver, has been in the United States for one year and can speak and understand English well enough to function in school. He has done well in his studies, carrying a 2.5 grade point average with his highest grades in literature and history courses. He struggled through the first semester of chemistry, however, with Ds and Fs on most tests, which were based on class lectures. His lab reports salvaged his grade because they were always of the highest quality — a fact that his teacher, Mr. Thompson, attributed mainly to the influence and help of Miguel's lab partner, Dave, the best student in the class.

When everyone was assigned a new lab partner for the second semester, Miguel was paired with Tim, who was failing the course. Miguel's lab reports, however, continued to be excellent, and Tim's also improved significantly. Mr. Thompson was puzzled by Miguel's performance.

How might Miguel's performance in chemistry class be explained?

_____

_____

_____

_____

_____

_____

_____

_____

Now, of the following, which best explains the situation?

1. Miguel does not listen attentively to the class lectures and does not, therefore, take adequate notes for the tests.
2. Miguel "freezes up" when taking tests.
3. Miguel learns better when he can discover things for himself and discuss his ideas with others. Thus, the lab environment is ideal for him.
4. Miguel lacks the analytic mind necessary to be successful in the study of science.
5. The lab sessions are less demanding than the material presented in class lectures.

Feedback on these alternatives can be found on page 91.

## Feedback on Critical Incidents

## Rationales for: The Model Minority

1. You chose number 1. Hong Kong, where Wellington comes from, is a highly urbanized environment. The majority of Chinese from the People's Republic come from a very different, often rural, setting. In addition, socioeconomic and class differences between Chinese from Hong Kong and Mainland China may also be at play. Mr. Fenwick has mistakenly put all Chinese into a single category, failing to make the finer distinctions necessary to more fully understand this group. This is the best response.
2. You chose number 2. We know that Mr. Fenwick has had extensive interaction with ethnic minorities in the school setting. There is a more appropriate response. Please choose again.
3. You chose number 3. Prior experience and expectations can often predispose one to expect certain behavior. In this case the text states that Mr. Fenwick did have certain

prior experiences with Chinese that were quite different from those he is having with Wellington. It may very well be that Mr. Fenwick has unrealistic expectations of Wellington given his prior experience. This answer is partially correct.

4. You chose number 4. There is no indication in the story that Mr. Fenwick has taken a personal dislike to Wellington. Please select an explanation that reflects possible intercultural interaction.

## Rationales for: Typical American Practice

1. While jealousy and resentment over grades are always possibilities, there is no evidence this is happening here. Please choose again.

2. Cultures differ in the amount of attention given to sojourners. Visitors to the United States frequently comment that Americans are polite during initial interaction but then seem indifferent at meeting the visitor a second or third time. For instance, foreign students may be introduced and made to feel welcome, but those same students seem to be forgotten a few days later. Keiko seems to be receiving this "typical" American treatment. It would help if Americans and all hosts tried to put themselves in the place of the newly arrived person and then try to make him or her feel really at home, especially by including the person in social activities. In some respects, Keiko has been accepted and treated as she would be if she were another American. Keiko will have to work slowly to develop a more intimate, small ingroup where she is one of the gang. This provides the best explanation.

3. This explanation has no basis in the narrative above. So far as we know, the faculty members were apparently sincere in their welcome and acted on their own initiative. Their behavior is the real problem, but their motives probably were not. Please choose again.

4. Most sojourners have some type of unrealistic expectation, and Keiko is probably no different. But she does not appear overly demanding of her hosts. Her puzzlement and withdrawal seem well founded and understandable. Look elsewhere for the real problem here.

## Rationales for: The Students Are Anxious, but Why?

1. You chose number 1. There is a grain of truth to this. For some students who work slowly, strict time limits can be unnerving. In addition, people from some cultures do not have the same orientation to time as others may. However, there is more going on in this case. Please choose again.

2. You chose number 2. This is the best response for these circumstances. By the time these students reached high school they may have had many negative expe-

riences with standardized tests, which tend to reflect white, middle-class culture and suburban school settings. Their expectations of failure may be quite high. While most probably could not verbalize the reasons for their reactions, they probably felt that they wouldn't do well and therefore may have tried to avoid the situation and/or relieve their tensions. This anxious behavior is what Ms. McConnell was seeing. If Ms. McConnell had been sensitive to the issue at hand, she would have directly addressed the students' anxiety about test taking. The fact that she did not, and that the students did not identify the cause of their uneasiness, was the direct cause of the students' undirected misbehavior. Teachers need to be sensitive to the anxieties of students who have regularly had the experience of receiving low grades and test scores.

3. You chose number 3. While this may be of concern to a few students, it does not realistically explain the generalized resistance Mary McConnell felt. Please choose again.

4. You chose number 4. On the contrary, students usually enjoy interruptions to the daily routine. They may not have enjoyed this particular type of interruption, however. There is a better alternative. Please select again.

## Rationales for: The Art Awards Ceremony

1. You chose number 1. Although Tony may have been overwhelmed by the attention and aware of Mr. Tarbell's position, there is really no indication that he was uncomfortable. Please choose again.

2. You chose number 2. Although Mr. Tarbell thought he was complimenting Tony, his use of language — specifically the phrase "uncanny ability to paint" — implies a stereotyping of blacks as not artistic. To a white student, he might have said, "You are a very talented young artist," — but Tony's ability to paint seems unnatural to him. Because of Mr. Tarbell's position Tony may have chosen to walk away rather than challenge him. You have selected the correct answer.

3. You chose number 3. His friends may have motioned to him although there is no indication of this is the story. Choose another response.

4. You chose number 4. Although there may be something uncomfortable about the situation, nothing in the story really shows that Tony was embarrassed or uncomfortable. Choose another response.

## Rationales for: The Missed Meeting

1. Mrs. Conant's concern seems sincere and well founded, and the parents seem to appreciate it since they were immediately agreeable to the conference. The problem lies elsewhere. Please choose again.

2. Although the parents were obviously late for the appointment, there is no evidence to support the notion that they were intentionally insensitive or that they lacked concern for their daughter's progress. While "time" may be the main problem here, this attribution of motives and feelings is not justified by the evidence.

3. The differing views of "time" held by Mrs. Conant and the parents are the roots of the problem and the best explanations of the hurt feelings on both sides. The working unit of time for European Americans tends to be a five-minute block. Mrs. Conant, therefore, would probably consider that a person who is two or three minutes late for a meeting need not apologize. After five minutes, however, a short apology would be expected. Being 15 minutes late, representing three unit blocks of time, would require a lengthy, sincere apology, or perhaps a phone call in advance.

   Not all cultures, however, place the same emphasis on time and punctuality as do Western cultures. Historical perspectives are important to Arab people. The working unit of time for many Arabs (as well as for Latinos and Native Americans, among other people) is a much longer block than it is for Westerners. Mrs. Conant and the parents are, therefore, victims of conflicting views of time and punctuality. This is the best response.

4. All the evidence suggests that Mrs. Conant is most agreeable to have conferences during her free period. Indeed, she initiates this meeting. Please choose again.

## Rationales for: Careful Preparation of Lectures

1. You chose alternative 1. Although there is an increasing body of knowledge and literature emerging that focuses on the adult learner and that should be utilized when planning instruction for adults, the students in this incident were not that much older than the students Robert was accustomed to teaching. These young farm workers would not require these kinds of modifications. Please select another response.

2. You chose alternative 2. Although these workers probably all speak Spanish, they also understand and regularly speak Standard English. This is not a critical factor here. Please select another alternative.

3. You chose alternative 3. It has been found that many Mexican American farm workers (as well as many other people from cultures without a long experience with a written language) typically teach each other and, therefore, learn in context rather than out of context. While Robert's professional training and experiences have stressed out-of-context learning of material (through books, films, lectures, and so forth), which would be applied at a later time, many people learn more and become more involved and motivated when taught in an in-context sit-

uation. An out-of-classroom, hands-on approach would probably facilitate their learning process. This is the best response.

4. You chose alternative 4. There is no indication that the workers resented Robert or the fact that he was introducing new machinery. In fact, the incident mentions that the workers were looking forward to using these machines. Please choose again.

## Rationales for: The Chemistry Lab

1. There is no evidence that Miguel does not pay attention or that he fails to take adequate notes. Please choose again.

2. Since Miguel has a 2.5 grade point avergae, he must be doing well in tests in some of his courses. Freezing up on tests is, therefore, probably not the reason for his performance in chemistry class.

3. Since Miguel does consistently well in lab work, he probably feels more comfortable and confident in such a "hands-on," "shared-responsibility" learning situation. The emphasis of lab work on activity, exploration, and group learning matches the learning style of Miguel's cultural background. This is the best answer.

4. Miguel's performance in lab work shows that he does have the analytic ability necessary to understand scientific concepts. This is not an adequate explanation for his performance. Please choose again.

5. No evidence indicates that the lab sessions are less demanding. Please choose another response.

# Observing Cultural Differences

## Purpose

To apply the 18-theme culture-general framework to casual observations made during interactions with others.

## Instructions

Make extended observations of yourself as well as others over the course of about a week. The focus of your observations should be on potential misunderstanding or miscommunication between people of different cultural backgrounds (remember that we define culture rather broadly). Record your observations as precisely as possible, identifying any and all of the culture-general themes that you believe apply. Finally, propose alternative explanations or attributions for the behavior you have observed from two (or more) perspectives. Use the following as a guide, but do not necessarily limit yourself to the space provided. You should make *at least* five different relevant observations. Make additional copies of this form if needed.

## Example

| Interaction as I Observed It | Cultural-General Theme(s) | Possible Attributions |
|---|---|---|
| Example: Two girls, one Mexican, the other Canadian European, discuss plans of what they will do Friday night. Mexican girl insists upon asking her parents' permission before making commitment to Canadian friend. | Family roles Individualism vs collectivism | Collectivist orientation (tendency for Mexicans). May require approval from others before taking action, whereas Canadian (individualistic tendency) is more comfortable making her own plans. |

| Interaction as I Observed It | Cultural-General Theme(s) | Possible Attributions |
| --- | --- | --- |
| | | |

| Interaction as I Observed It | Cultural-General Theme(s) | Possible Attributions |
| --- | --- | --- |
| | | |

| Interaction as I Observed It | Cultural-General Theme(s) | Possible Attributions |
| --- | --- | --- |
| | | |

## Activity 15

# Learning About Others

## Purpose

To learn about cultural differences by interviewing someone from a different culture or ethnic group while applying concepts from the culture-general framework.

## Instructions

Find someone from a culture different from your own to interview (preferably some-one outside your immediate and known peer group). Try to choose someone you think will have different attitudes, opinions, and experiences from yourself. Choose some questions from the list that follows, or develop some of your own. Before you inter-view the person, answer the questions for yourself. For each of the questions, follow up with "Why?" in order to explore underlying values. Take notes on the responses. Discuss the questions and the "why" with the other person until you have found at least five major areas where there are clear differences between your answer and the other person's. Also be sure to identify five major areas where you are in agreement with one another. Prepare a short paper or presentation that summarizes your findings.

a. Whom should you obey? Why?

b. Who makes decisions (at home, in school, in the community)? Why?

c. How should you behave with others (elders, children, neighbors)? Why?

d. Whom should you respect? How do you show respect? Why?

e. How should you act in public so you bring credit or honor to your family? Why?

f. What does it mean to be successful in life? Why?

g. Whom should you trust? Why?

h. What are the signs of success? Why?

i. What provides "security" in life? Why?

j. Who should your friends be? Who decides? Why?

k. Where, and with whom, should you live? Why?

l. Whom should you marry? At about what age? Who decides? Why?

m. What is expected of children when they are young? Why?

n. What should you depend on others for? Why?

o. When should you be self-sufficient, if ever? Why?

p. What should you expose to others, and what should be kept private? Why?

q. How should you plan for your future? Why?

r. What should be remembered from your heritage? Why?

s. What was better when you were younger or during your parents' youth? Why?

t. What do you wish for your children that you could not have? Why?

**What did you learn about the other person that is significantly different from you? How might this knowledge affect the interviewee as a learner? You as a teacher?**

_____

_____

_____

_____

_____

_____

_____

_____

_____

_____

**What did you learn about the other person that is similar to you? Were you surprised by this? How might this knowledge affect you as a teacher?**

_____

_____

_____

_____

_____

_____

_____

_____

_____

# Community Scan: Analyzing Available Resources That Support Multicultural Education

## Purpose

To develop a deeper understanding of a local community in terms of available resources that support as well as hinder the goals and objectives of multicultural education.

## Instructions

Plan to survey a community over a period of a few days by studying a small section or neighborhood at a time. You may do this activity individually, but it is better if it can be accomplished in small groups. If done in small groups, each group should take responsibility for a different neighborhood, but be certain to select neighborhoods that all serve a common school. Later, share your findings with others so all may gain a more complete understanding of the area, what influences children are exposed to, and what resources might be available to educators.

1. Before you begin your observation, make a list of the things you expect to find that support multicultural education as well as those that pose threats or obstacles.

   _____

   _____

   _____

   _____

   _____

2. Begin by walking around the area you are to analyze. What resources do you find that may support efforts to increase understanding of diversity and multicultural education? For instance, what ethnic groups are present? What languages are spoken? What global links are evident? What places of worship exist? What ethnic restaurants and ethnic food stores can be found? What community services exist to assist the poor, the elderly, or the disabled?

_____

_____

_____

_____

_____

_____

3. Interview storeowners and shopkeepers in the neighborhood. What are their impressions of the cultural diversity in the community? How is diversity an asset or an obstacle to them? What is their impression of the role schools play in addressing issues of diversity?

_____

_____

_____

_____

_____

_____

4. What community resources or industries can you identify that may offer possible school-community linkages or other ways to relate the curriculum to the community and the environment?

_____

_____

_____

_____

_____

5.  What unique cultural experiences and resources do you think children will bring with them to school as a result of growing up in this community? How might you build upon these in the classroom and school?

 

_____

_____

_____

_____

_____

_____

6.  What unique aspects of this community do you think might hinder a school's ability to effectively address multicultural or diversity education? How might you overcome these?

 

_____

_____

_____

_____

_____

_____

7.  What aspects of community life do you still have questions about? How might you go about finding the answers to these?

 

_____

_____

_____

_____

_____

_____

8. Describe any surprises, unexpected outcomes, or concerns about your community scan.

_____

_____

_____

_____

_____

_____

_____

_____

_____

_____

_____

_____

## Activity 17

# Stereotypes and Their Impact on
# Interaction and Learning

## Purpose

To recognize stereotypes of various groups and how they affect interaction and learning.

## Instructions

Stereotypes refer to a belief about the personal attributes of individuals based on the inaccurate generalizations used to describe all members of a group, thus ignoring individual differences. Try to identify at least three stereotypes of each group identified on the following pages, state the source of these stereotypes, and explain how they affect interaction and learning.

| Group | Example of the stereotype | Its source | How it affects interaction and learning |
|---|---|---|---|
| lesbians and gay men | such people are interested in me as a sexual object. | friends | fear of interaction |
| | | | |
| | | | |
| | | | |

| Group | Example of the stereotype | Its source | How it affects interaction and learning |
|---|---|---|---|
| Latinos/ Hispanics | Latino men are all macho | movies/TV | fear that female child (or my student) will be treated as a second-class citizen |
|  |  |  |  |
|  |  |  |  |
|  |  |  |  |

| Group | Example of the stereotype | Its source | How it affects interaction and learning |
|---|---|---|---|
| Asian | Asian women are submissive | movies/TV | may not be offered positions of power and authority |
|  |  |  |  |
|  |  |  |  |
|  |  |  |  |

**Continue in this manner, identifying a group, generating a list of stereotypes, and analyzing their impact on interaction and learning. You might include such groups as African Americans, European Americans, Catholics, teenagers, the elderly, and so forth.**

| Group | Example of the stereotype | Its source | How it affects interaction and learning |
|---|---|---|---|
|  |  |  |  |
|  |  |  |  |
|  |  |  |  |

## Reflection

Working in small groups, compare patterns of similarity and difference of stereotypes believed to be held about each group. Because there tends to be much emotion surrounding stereotypes, it is not necessary to indicate whether or not you agree with the stereotype — just that you identify it as one you believe to be common about the group.

How did you feel while completing this activity?

_____

_____

_____

_____

_____

How did actual group members of any of the racial, cultural, or ethnic groups mentioned respond to the results as well as the subsequent discussion?

_____

_____

_____

_____

_____

What have been the major sources of the stereotypes?

_____

_____

_____

_____

_____

In what ways have stereotypes affected intercultural interaction?

_____

_____

_____

_____

_____

In what ways might stereotypes affect learning?

_____

_____

_____

_____

_____

What might teachers do to help reduce the likelihood that students will use stereo-types?

_____

_____

_____

_____

_____

# Privilege: The Invisible Knapsack

## Purpose

To explore institutional biases, the oftentimes unexamined privileges held by members of certain groups, typically able-bodied, heterosexual, European Americans, that enables them to move with relative ease throughout society.

## Instructions

In her paper, *White Privilege and Male Privilege*, Peggy McIntosh (1988) uses racism as a way to demonstrate the nature and depth of institutional bias people typically take for granted in society. Explore the benefits certain groups have in society by responding to the following questions.

1. Begin by thinking about some of the benefits you think European Americans may have in American society and take for granted that non-whites may not have. Before reviewing McIntosh's list, try to identify at least five privileges you think would be included on the list:

   _____

   _____

   _____

   _____

   _____

2. Now, compare your results with some of the following from McIntosh's original list. McIntosh identified such privileges of whites as:

   • When they go into stores, they won't automatically be viewed as potential shoplifters.
   • When they go to college, they won't automatically be thought of in terms of "affirmative action" admits (or "affirmative action" hires if this is a workplace).
   • When they apply for a bank loan, they won't automatically be viewed as a bad credit risk.

- When they attend school or begin a new job, they will find role models of similar background.
- When they apply for a job, the people in power will be of their race.
- When they speak up in a group, they will not be assumed to be speaking on behalf of an entire community, but of themselves.
- When they study history in school, they will learn about their own heritage.
- When they walk down a street at night they will not be perceived as a threat.

Now that you have read some of McIntosh's original list, can you think of any other privileges that may exist for whites in society?

_____

_____

_____

_____

_____

3. The same exercise can be completed to examine institutional biases against many groups in society, such as the elderly, gays and lesbians, the disabled, or the poor. It may be easier to generate a list if you are a member of a particular group; however, this is not always the case. In some instances, people may attribute difficulties or barriers to their own shortcomings or lack of ability, and they may be invisible even to themselves.

Now, identify another group in society and generate at least five examples of "invisible" barriers that may confront its members.

Group: _____

_____

_____

_____

_____

_____

_____

_____

4. Many people who enjoy privileges fail to recognize them. While they may understand that slavery and a lack of voting rights for African Americans and women are forms of institutional discrimination, they may falsely assume that since these wrongs have been corrected society as a whole is fair and equal. A beginning step at dismantling institutional discrimination is to do your own consciousness-raising. If you are discriminated against, it is important to gain as much clarity on the situation as possible. If you are a beneficiary of the system, you should begin to examine ways in which you can change things.

What are some things that you can do, both personally and professionally, to address such issues?

_____

_____

_____

_____

_____

_____

_____

_____

_____

(adapted from Summerfield, 1997)

# Interviewing Non-Native English Speakers about Their Experiences in This Country

## Purpose

To raise awareness and sensitivity, and to learn about the problems faced by new speakers of English.

## Instructions

Interview a person who first came to the United States speaking limited or no English. This person might be an international student on campus, or a student and/or parent who came to the United States speaking minimal English (feel free to adjust the questions accordingly to accommodate the person you are interviewing).

1. Describe some of the initial difficulties or problems you encountered when you first arrived in this country. To what would you attribute the problems?

   _____

   _____

   _____

   _____

   _____

   _____

2. What significant cultural differences did you encounter in the early stages of your adjustment to this country? How did you overcome these?

   _____

   _____

   _____

   _____

   _____

   _____

3. What primary language did you speak before coming to the United States? Describe your competency as a speaker of your home language. Describe your competency as a speaker of English today.

_____

_____

_____

_____

_____

_____

4. What communication problems did you experience when you first came to this country? How did you handle these?

_____

_____

_____

_____

_____

_____

5. What kinds of communication difficulties, if any, do you or your children currently face?

_____

_____

_____

_____

_____

_____

6. What might people (or schools and/or teachers if interviewing a child or parent) in the United States do that would help to reduce adjustment and communication difficulties for new immigrants?

_____

_____

_____

_____

_____

_____

_____

7. What messages do you have for other non-English speakers that might make their adjustment and communication easier?

_____

_____

_____

_____

_____

_____

_____

*In conclusion*: What can you conclude about communication, culture shock, and adjustment that would be useful for teachers?

_____

_____

_____

_____

_____

_____

_____

# What Does It Feel Like to Be Excluded?

## Purpose

To develop empathy by imagining what it might be like to be excluded or discriminated against, and to propose possible responses.

## Instructions

Developing an understanding of the experience of others in a pluralistic society is critical if teachers and students are to develop a fuller knowledge of culture and its various forms. One way to develop such a skill is to listen to the voices of individuals who have felt excluded from the mainstream for one reason or another—perhaps due to overt racism; subtle, institutional racism; general ignorance; subtle pressure; or genuine dislike. Read the following quotes and try to identify one or two feelings associated with them. Then consider what you as a teacher might say and do in response (adapted from an exercise developed by Beth Swadener).

**Low-income mother:** "My son understands that we have no money the last week of each month, and yet he was pressured by his teacher to have a new workbook by the next class. When we could not afford it that week he was made to sit out of class. The teacher said, "Everyone else remembered to get their book, why didn't you?"

As the mother, I feel

_____

_____

_____

As a teacher, I might

_____

_____

_____

**Jewish parent:** "Last year our daughter asked me, 'Could we have a Christmas tree and just not use it?'"

As the parent, I feel

_____

_____

_____

As a teacher, I might

_____

_____

_____

**Chinese parent:** "My daughter asked me, 'Can I have blonde hair? It's better to be blonde.'"

As the parent, I feel

_____

_____

_____

As a teacher, I might

_____

_____

_____

**Native American parent:** "The schools continue to miseducate my son. The images he has of native people are limited, and there is virtually no relevant Native American history taught in his school."

As the parent, I feel

_____

_____

_____

As a teacher, I might

_____

_____

_____

**Islamic parent:** "My child's school has many Christian-based activities and has never even recognized that some of the students are not Christian."

As the parent, I feel

_____

_____

_____

As a teacher, I might

_____

_____

_____

**Single parent mother:** "I feel that all my son's behavior at school is blamed on the fact that I'm a single parent, and that many judgments about our family are made based on no other evidence than our 'single-parent family' status."

As the mother, I feel

_____

_____

_____

As a teacher, I might

_____

_____

_____

**Vietnamese parent:** (translated from Vietnamese) "My children speak and read better English than I do. It is so hard when lots of letters and information come home from school in English. I also feel that my children are losing respect for their parents and elders in this country."

As the parent, I feel

_____

_____

_____

As a teacher, I might

_____

_____

_____

Extend this activity by collecting some of your own quotes from statements by children, parents, and other community members who represent diverse groups and who have felt excluded. Record three examples below.

_____

_____

_____

_____

_____

_____

_____

_____

_____

_____

_____

_____

_____

_____

# Gender Role Socialization

## Purpose

To identify some of the ways males and females are differentially socialized in mainstream American society.

## Instructions

The following are generalizations concerning gender role socialization in American society. Provide an example of each, either from your own experience or from what you have witnessed in society in general. Then respond to the reflective questions.

| A Woman Is Taught | My Example | A Man Is Taught | My Example |
|---|---|---|---|
| To do what she is asked | _____ | To control | _____ |
| To be pleasing to a man | _____ | To score, to achieve | _____ |
| To hurt no one's feelings | _____ | To pursue goals, to take charge | _____ |
| To look good | _____ | To discuss women's bodies | _____ |
| To be taken care of | _____ | To have a dream | _____ |
| To compete for male attention | _____ | To work as a team | _____ |
| To care for others before herself | _____ | To take risks and challenges | _____ |
| To follow rules | _____ | To make rules and decisions | _____ |
| To let others make choices | _____ | To put women on a pedestal | _____ |
| To be friendly, helpful | _____ | To expect service from women | _____ |

Which of these are advantages in American society?

_____

_____

_____

_____

_____

_____

_____

Which of these are disadvantages in American society?

_____

_____

_____

_____

_____

_____

_____

How are some of these perpetuated in schools?

_____

_____

_____

_____

_____

_____

_____

## Activity 22

# Observing Gender Differences

## Purpose

To develop a deeper understanding of the influence gender plays in development, socialization, and education.

## Instructions

Read the following story, which you may have already heard. Then do the following activities and respond to the reflective questions that follow.

A father and his son were in a terrible automobile accident. They were injured so severely that they were taken to different hospitals. The son required immediate surgery, so a surgeon was called in. The surgeon walked into the operating room, took one look at the patient, and said, "I can't operate on this boy. This boy is my son!" How can this be?

It should be obvious to you that the surgeon was the boy's mother. For the most part, when we think of surgeons or doctors in general, most of us do not expect them to be women. Although much has been written and done in recent years to change the way people think about gender and the various roles people adopt, people's thinking along these lines tend to be rather static. Far too many people still think of men as managers, administrators, and leaders and women as subordinates, holding other stereotypic roles (e.g., secretaries, nurses, and oftentimes teachers).

The following activities will help you to gain a deeper picture of the influence gender plays in development, socialization, and education.

A. Arrange to do observations of children's play behavior at a nearby school, both of preschool and elementary children. Summarize your observations by responding to the following questions.

*When observing preschool boys and girls, what gender differences are you able to observe? Think of the way children act, their choices of play activities as well as playmates, and their responses to various stimuli.*

_____

_____

_____

_____

_____

*Do a similar comparison of elementary-aged children (you may wish to restrict this to specific age groups, such as seven- and eight-year-olds, nine- and ten-year-olds, etc.). What do you notice?*

_____

_____

_____

_____

_____

_____

*What happens when you ask boys and girls to play with a toy or game typically assigned to the other sex?*

_____

_____

_____

_____

_____

_____

B. Using a week's worth of your campus or local newspaper, circle every headline in which females or males are mentioned. Compare the number of mentions of each. Compare the number of roles associated with males and females (e.g., husband, wife, banker, politician, daughter, son, athlete, etc.). In what sections of the paper are males and females referred to most often? Is there a difference between the campus newspaper, the local paper, a national paper? What generalizations are you able to make given your observations?

_____

_____

_____

_____

_____

_____

C. Examine the textbooks used in teacher education and arts and sciences. Look for evidence of gender bias discussed or presented in various chapters. One interesting activity is to count and compare the number of males and females listed in the index. Do the same for various textbooks used in elementary and secondary schools. What generalizations are you able to make given your observations?

_____

_____

_____

_____

_____

D. Make a comparison of the chores you were expected to do at home as you were growing up. If you have brothers or sisters, were their chores similar or different? If you were an only child, or had only siblings of the same sex, talk to someone else who had siblings of the opposite sex. How were your chores similar or different? What does this suggest?

_____

_____

_____

_____

_____

E.  Do a comparison study among your classmates in terms of the number and kinds of math and science courses each took in high school. Is there any difference between the males and the females? Can people describe the reasons for taking or not taking math and science courses? Compare reasons of males versus those of females. What generalizations are you able to make given your observations?

_____

_____

_____

_____

_____

_____

# The Plight of Women on a Global Scale

## Purpose

To become better informed about the experience of women on a global scale and to project oneself into the experience of the other.

## Instructions

Read and respond to the following.

The majority of the information we have about people in the world (including most of the social and behavioral science research) has been based on the experience of males, or is presented in gender-neutral language (although it still may be based on the experience of males. See Carol Gilligan's [1983] book, *In A Different Voice*, to understand how the experience of females is oftentimes quite different than that of males and from that reported in much of the research literature). Following is some information about women in the world that you might consider (adapted from Drum, Hughes and Otero, 1994):

a. While women make up more than half of the world's population, they do two-thirds of the world's work, both paid and unpaid, and receive only one-tenth of the world's wages.

b. Rural women account for more than half of the food produced in the developing world, and for as much as 80 percent of the food production in Africa.

c. The hourly wages of working women in the manufacturing industry are on average three-fourths those earned by men.

d. In the United States, on the average, women earn 70 percent of each dollar earned by men.

e. In 1950, there were 27 million more boys than girls enrolled in schools worldwide. Currently there are 80 million more boys than girls enrolled in schools.

f. Nutritional anemia afflicts half of all women of childbearing age in developing countries, compared with less than 7 percent of women of childbearing age in developed countries.

g. In the developing world, two-thirds of the women over the age of 25 (and about one-half of the men) have never been to school.

h. Ten of the eleven oldest democracies in the world did not grant women the right to vote until the twentieth century. The first to establish electoral equality was New Zealand in 1893. The last to establish electoral equality was Switzerland in 1971.

i. Women represent 50 percent of the voting population in the world but hold only 10 percent of the seats in national legislatures.

What do you think about and feel when you read these statistics?

_____

_____

_____

_____

_____

If you could choose to be any gender, which would you choose to be and why?

_____

_____

_____

_____

_____

Which gender would you choose if you lived in the Third World and why?

_____

_____

_____

_____

_____

When do either women or men encounter injustice as a result of their gender?

_____

_____

_____

_____

_____

If you could choose a gender for your child, which would you choose and why?

_____

_____

_____

_____

_____

Now imagine you are of the opposite gender. How might your answers to these questions be different?

_____

_____

_____

_____

_____

_____

# Sexual Orientation: A Matter of Experience?

## Purpose

To examine potential classroom situations that reflect others' as well as your own responses to issues surrounding sexual orientation.

## Instructions

The term sexual orientation refers to the preference one exhibits in terms of sexual partners. There is increasing evidence that one's sexual orientation is genetically based; that is, it may be "hard-wired" into the individual, and therefore resistant, if not impossible, to change. Other beliefs attribute early experience to later sexual preference. Regardless of the explanation you are most comfortable with, in your role as an educator you will encounter situations that will require your action and intervention on behalf of a child, either in making accurate attributions concerning a child's behavior at a given moment, or on behalf of a child who is experiencing strained relationships with her or his peers.

How would you explain the following scenarios to the concerned individual?

a. Four-year-old Jeremy heads right to the doll corner as soon as he arrives at the day care center each morning. His father is concerned that this behavior is not appropriate for a little boy. How would you respond to the father?

_____

_____

_____

_____

_____

_____

_____

_____

_____

b. Seventeen-year-old Patricia (who prefers to be called Pat) wears her hair cut very short and tends to dress like the boys. You walk by a group of her female classmates and hear them refer to her as a lesbian. How would you respond to this group of girls?

_____

_____

_____

_____

_____

_____

_____

_____

_____

c. Five-year-old Suzanne plays with blocks and trucks during most of her free time in kindergarten. Her mother asks you if this is "normal" behavior? How would you respond to the mother?

_____

_____

_____

_____

_____

_____

_____

_____

_____

d. In addition to his theater performances, thirteen-year-old Robert takes ballet classes three days a week after school. Other boys often ridicule him in class. He comes to you and asks you to intervene. What would you suggest to Robert?

_____

_____

_____

_____

_____

_____

_____

_____

_____

_____

_____

What would you say to the other boys in Robert's class?

_____

_____

_____

_____

_____

_____

_____

_____

_____

_____

_____

e. Fifteen-year-old Shauna, who has few friends, lifts weights and seeks out all the opportunities she can to play typical boys' sports. She has also been having conflicting and confusing sexual feelings. She comes to you after school one day, initially to seek your advice about what to do about friends, but soon begins to talk about her confusion and fear of talking to her parents. What advice would you give her?

_____

_____

_____

_____

_____

_____

_____

_____

_____

_____

f. Sixteen-year-old Joseph's stated goal in life is to become a nurse. You overhear a group of boys teasing him and laughing about his "gay" behavior. You find Joseph sulking in a corner of the room and approach him. What do you say to him?

_____

_____

_____

_____

_____

_____

_____

_____

_____

_____

Reflect upon your responses to the above scenarios. Do you notice any patterns in the way you answered the questions? Did you respond differently to the scenarios involving girls than you did for the scenarios involving boys? Did you respond differently to parents than you did to the child? If so, to what do you attribute this?

_____

_____

_____

_____

_____

_____

_____

_____

_____

_____

_____

_____

_____

_____

_____

_____

_____

_____

_____

_____

_____

_____

# The Student with Special Needs

## Purpose

To assist future teachers with gaining greater understanding and insight into the probable expectations and responsibilities toward children with special needs.

## Instructions

Full inclusion of all children in all classrooms is likely to be a major emphasis in the years to come, thus making it essential that all teachers are well versed in ways to accommodate the needs of children with special needs. The following exercises will assist you in developing a greater understanding of your role and responsibilities.

A. Arrange to do an observation of a classroom that has children who have special needs. What do you notice about the manner in which the teacher interacts with the children who have special needs compared with those without special needs? What needs do the children seem to have that are unique to this group? Common to other children? What modifications in instructional approach are evident?

_____

_____

_____

_____

_____

_____

_____

_____

_____

_____

_____

_____

B. Interview a parent of a child who receives special educational services. In what ways has the child been helped? What improvements are still needed in the education the child receives? What recommendations does the parent have for you, as a future teacher, regarding what you might provide for children who have special needs?

_____

_____

_____

_____

_____

_____

_____

_____

_____

_____

C. Interview a teacher, focusing on how she or he has been affected by educational policy directed at children with special needs. What modifications has the teacher made in teaching? What special preparation has she or he received to help make the necessary changes? What does the teacher still feel is needed?

_____

_____

_____

_____

_____

_____

_____

_____

_____

_____

D. Ask to observe a conference where an Individual Educational Plan (IEP) is developed for a student with special needs. Analyze the perspectives and needs of each of the parties at the meeting. What concerns did parents address? Teachers? Administrators? Psychologists? Students? What concerns did you have that were not addressed?

_____

_____

_____

_____

_____

_____

_____

_____

_____

_____

_____

# Understanding Religious Diversity

## Purpose

To assist you with gaining greater understanding and reducing stereotypes of the major religions that may be encountered in schools and communities.

## Instructions

Derive a series of interview questions using the guidelines below. Then conduct interviews with individuals who represent religions other than your own.

A. In small groups, generate potential interview questions you could use to help gain greater understanding and reduce misperceptions about religions other than your own.

B. Discuss these questions with the class and determine which among them will help to uncover stereotypes, attitudes, perceptions and misperceptions of a particular group.

C. Agree as a class upon 5 to 7 questions that will generate the most useful information.

D. Using the same questions, individually or in pairs, interview at least two individuals from religious groups other than your own. You should seek to find representatives from at least the five major world religions (Christianity, Judaism, Islam, Buddhism, and Hinduism), as well as any other groups of interest and available in your region.

E. Individually, summarize key points of your interviews.

F.  As a class, discuss the following:

a.  Did the questions you asked provide you with the information you had hoped for?

b.  Discuss at least one response that you found surprising or interesting. What did you find especially intriguing about this response?

c.  Was there anything the interviewee said that led you to reconsider any of your views?

d.  Did you learn anything significant from the interviewee about the religion?

e.  Were any stereotypes you might have held about this religion challenged?

f.  Now that the interviews are complete, are there any questions you wish you had asked?

g.  What did you learn in this exercise that will impact your teaching?

# Institutional Discrimination: Social Class in Focus

## Purpose

To distinguish between individual and institutional practices that may discriminate against certain social classes.

## Instructions

Institutional discrimination refers to policies and practices of institutions that allow certain discriminatory practices to persist. Below you will be presented with a number of situations. You will be asked to determine if these policies or practices systematically privilege members of certain groups while discriminating against members of other groups. Complete the three questions that follow for each of the following that you determine to be an example of institutional discrimination.

1. Children of teachers employed in this private school receive free tuition.

    Is this an example of discrimination?    _____ Yes    _____ No

    a. Against which groups, if any, might this policy discriminate?

    _____

    _____

    _____

    b. What is the purpose of the policy?

    _____

    _____

    _____

    c. If the purpose is valid, how else might it be achieved?

    _____

    _____

    _____

2. A local religious school offers reduced tuition for members of its faith.

Is this an example of discrimination?     _____ Yes     _____ No

   a. Against which groups, if any, might this policy discriminate?

_____

_____

_____

   b. What is the purpose of the policy?

_____

_____

_____

   c. If the purpose is valid, how else might it be achieved?

_____

_____

_____

3. Because a recent school levy failed, a new school policy states that children who wish to participate in sports or musical performing groups must pay for their own uniforms.

Is this an example of discrimination?     _____ Yes     _____ No

   a. Against which groups, if any, might this policy discriminate?

_____

_____

_____

   b. What is the purpose of the policy?

_____

_____

_____

c. If the purpose is valid, how else might it be achieved?

_____

_____

_____

4. A teacher awards ten points out of 100 to boys who wear a jacket and tie and girls who wear a full-length dress during an oral presentation as part of the final grade in a business speech class.

Is this an example of discrimination?    _____ Yes    _____ No

a. Against which groups, if any, might this policy discriminate?

_____

_____

_____

b. What is the purpose of the policy?

_____

_____

_____

c. If the purpose is valid, how else might it be achieved?

_____

_____

_____

# Writing Your Own Critical Incidents

## Purpose

To develop skill in writing critical incidents that can be used to instruct others about issues related to diversity in the school context.

## Instructions

The critical incident is a short narrative describing a situation where two or more individuals from different cultural groups interact in order to achieve some goal. Differences due to cultural background, orientation, perspective, communication style, learning style, and so forth may result in some conflict or problem emerging with the situation generally going unresolved. The reader is asked to select, from a number of alternatives, the one that best explains the problem. The general approach to preparing critical incidents is as follows:

1. Identify relevant themes or issues for your purposes. You may select from the 18-theme cultural-general framework, or identify specific issues of relevance to your needs. Remember, you wish to use the incident to teach others about a cultural issue or theme underlying the incident, not merely to relate the story.

2. Generate episodes by identifying incidents through personal experience, interviews with others, reading the research and/or ethnographic literature, or observation and analysis. You may wish to use your observations from Activity 14 to form the basis of your incidents.

3. Construct episodes or stories, being certain to include only relevant information; verifying content; refining generalizations, abstractions, and specifics; and speaking to your intended audience. The resulting incident should be clear, concise, straightforward, interesting, and believable, while maintaining the original conflict situation.

4. Elicit attributions by identifying different interpretations (attributions) of the incident through interviews, ethnographic data, and open-ended questions completed by experienced and inexperienced individuals.

5. Select attributions to use.

6. Complete the critical incident with feedback and explanations, remembering that it is in the explanation that relevant cultural knowledge can be transmitted.

Now prepare three or four critical incidents that illuminate one or more of the 18 culture-general themes. Have the rough drafts of your incidents reviewed by others who can provide critical feedback to make sure they are clear, plausible, and easily understood.

# part three

# Modifying Curriculum and Instruction to Address the Goals of Diversity

## Activity 29

# Future's Window

## Purpose

To project the needs of individuals and society in the years ahead, and to examine what this means for educators.

## Instructions

In this activity you are to become a futurist and project into the future—both your own as well as that of the world. The work area below is divided into quadrants, the top half representing "The Self" and the bottom half representing "The World." The left side of each half represents "5 years" while the right half represents "20 years" into the future. You are to make at least five entries in each quadrant; things you expect to have accomplished or to be dealing with in 5 years and in 20 years, and things you expect the world to be confronting, both in 5 as well as 20 years. Do not record what you wish will happen, but what you predict will occur based on what you see happening today. Do this activity alone at first. If you are doing this in a group setting, after a short while, share your responses with others and compile a group list.

| *Self—5 years* | *Self—20 years* |
| --- | --- |
| | |

| *World—5 years* | *World—20 years* |
| --- | --- |
| | |

## Questions to Ponder

Look closely at what is on your list, or, if you have done this activity in a group, look closely at the compilation. What messages seem to jump out at you as you look closely at the response patterns? Do not be surprised if quick responses do not emerge. Take some time to analyze the similarities as well as the differences in the columns. What generalizations seem to emerge?

_____

_____

_____

_____

_____

_____

_____

_____

What questions do you have as a result of the generalizations you observed?

_____

_____

_____

_____

_____

_____

_____

_____

_____

As people analyze their responses it is not uncommon to say something like, "It seems as if things will be quite nice and easy for individuals but there will still be problems in the world." This is a critical observation. If you have not already made this observation yourself, please consider it for a moment. Does such a statement hold true for your responses to the above task?

Let's assume that you can safely make the same observation and statement given the responses on your list. What is the responsibility one has to others? Why do you think it is that, in general, people project their own future to be fine even when the rest of the world continues to face problems and challenges?

_____

_____

_____

_____

_____

_____

_____

_____

_____

_____

_____

_____

Discuss your responses to the above with others in a group. Do not be surprised if there is much disagreement over people's responses.

Next, look closely at your projections for the world. What generalizations seem to stand out as you analyze this information?

_____

_____

_____

_____

_____

_____

_____

_____

_____

_____

Which of the following statements can you agree with given the projections you have made for the world? Check one.

_____ The issues that the world will face seem quite pessimistic and insurmountable.

_____ The issues that the world will face seem complex but generally will be resolved.

It is often said that each individual can and must do her or his own part to help improve the bigger picture. All of the problems the world will face, whether they are in fact solved or not, will require the coordinated efforts of many different people from many different career and cultural backgrounds, who are able to work together. The problems of the world are such that they will be solved by the coordinated efforts of many different people and nations, or they will not be solved at all.

What is the role of education in helping people develop the ability to solve the problems that you believe the world will face?

_____

_____

_____

_____

_____

_____

What are some things you can do through your teaching that will help your students develop the awareness, knowledge, and skills necessary to collaborate with others whose ways of interacting and values may be quite different from their own?

_____

_____

_____

_____

_____

_____

_____

_____

# Ethnic Literacy Test: A Cultural Perspective
# Differentiating Stereotypes from Generalizations

## Purpose

To examine your knowledge of culture-specific information about certain ethnic groups within the United States and how this might impact teaching and learning.

## Instructions

This exercise has two parts. In Part One, place a checkmark along the continuum that corresponds to the extent to which you agree or disagree with the following statements. Qualify your response in the space below. In Part Two, you will be given additional information and asked to consider the educational implications of this culture-specific knowledge.

## Communication Differences

1. A newly arrived Mexican American child may have difficulty in reading words that begin with two consonants.

| strongly agree | tend to agree | unsure | tend to disagree | strongly disagree |
|---|---|---|---|---|

Rationale:

_____

_____

_____

2. Non-standard English, such as Ebonics, is a language system that has rules.

| strongly agree | tend to agree | unsure | tend to disagree | strongly disagree |
| --- | --- | --- | --- | --- |

Rationale:

_____

_____

_____

3. Many Appalachians form some possessive pronouns by adding n.

| strongly agree | tend to agree | unsure | tend to disagree | strongly disagree |
| --- | --- | --- | --- | --- |

Rationale:

_____

_____

_____

4. Ebonics, sometimes known as Black English, is a synonym for Black slang.

| strongly agree | tend to agree | unsure | tend to disagree | strongly disagree |
| --- | --- | --- | --- | --- |

Rationale:

_____

_____

_____

5. Vietnamese children may experience problems in spelling words that end with a double consonant.

| strongly agree | tend to agree | unsure | tend to disagree | strongly disagree |
| --- | --- | --- | --- | --- |

Rationale:

_____

_____

_____

6. Vietnamese children would have little difficulty reading polysyllabic words.

| strongly agree | tend to agree | unsure | tend to disagree | strongly disagree |
| --- | --- | --- | --- | --- |

Rationale:

_____

_____

_____

7. All Native Americans speak basically the same language.

| strongly agree | tend to agree | unsure | tend to disagree | strongly disagree |
| --- | --- | --- | --- | --- |

Rationale:

_____

_____

_____

8. Touching by a teacher and a Mexican American student results in lowered academic achievement.

| strongly agree | tend to agree | unsure | tend to disagree | strongly disagree |
|---|---|---|---|---|

Rationale:

_____

_____

_____

9. Touching the head of a Thai student signals respect.

| strongly agree | tend to agree | unsure | tend to disagree | strongly disagree |
|---|---|---|---|---|

Rationale:

_____

_____

_____

10. African Americans may interrupt a speaker with encouraging remarks.

| strongly agree | tend to agree | unsure | tend to disagree | strongly disagree |
|---|---|---|---|---|

Rationale:

_____

_____

_____

# Value Orientations

1. Native Americans' concept of time is the same as mainstream European Americans' concept of time.

| strongly agree | tend to agree | unsure | tend to disagree | strongly disagree |
| --- | --- | --- | --- | --- |

Rationale:

_____

_____

_____

2. Mexican American religious beliefs include the concept of fatalism.

| strongly agree | tend to agree | unsure | tend to disagree | strongly disagree |
| --- | --- | --- | --- | --- |

Rationale:

_____

_____

_____

3. Appalachians have strong kinship bonds.

| strongly agree | tend to agree | unsure | tend to disagree | strongly disagree |
| --- | --- | --- | --- | --- |

Rationale:

_____

_____

_____

4. African Americans have a strong work orientation.

| strongly agree | tend to agree | unsure | tend to disagree | strongly disagree |
| --- | --- | --- | --- | --- |

Rationale:

_____

_____

_____

5. Native Americans usually prefer public rather than private recognition.

| strongly agree | tend to agree | unsure | tend to disagree | strongly disagree |
| --- | --- | --- | --- | --- |

Rationale:

_____

_____

_____

6. Mexican American students generally desire to work alone rather than with a group.

| strongly agree | tend to agree | unsure | tend to disagree | strongly disagree |
| --- | --- | --- | --- | --- |

Rationale:

_____

_____

_____

7. Appalachians adapt easily to urban life.

| strongly agree | tend to agree | unsure | tend to disagree | strongly disagree |
| --- | --- | --- | --- | --- |

Rationale:

_____

_____

_____

8. African Americans tend to be deeply religious.

| strongly agree | tend to agree | unsure | tend to disagree | strongly disagree |
| --- | --- | --- | --- | --- |

Rationale:

_____

_____

_____

9. For some African Americans, to avoid eye contact with authority figures is a sign of disrespect.

| strongly agree | tend to agree | unsure | tend to disagree | strongly disagree |
| --- | --- | --- | --- | --- |

Rationale:

_____

_____

_____

10. Among Native Americans, the concept of private ownership is strong.

| strongly agree | tend to agree | unsure | tend to disagree | strongly disagree |
|---|---|---|---|---|

Rationale:

_____

_____

_____

## Family Structures and Lifestyles

1. The African American family is matriarchal.

| strongly agree | tend to agree | unsure | tend to disagree | strongly disagree |
|---|---|---|---|---|

Rationale:

_____

_____

_____

2. The majority of Appalachian families are nuclear.

| strongly agree | tend to agree | unsure | tend to disagree | strongly disagree |
|---|---|---|---|---|

Rationale:

_____

_____

_____

3. The Appalachian family tends to be patriarchal, and boys are favored.

| strongly agree | tend to agree | unsure | tend to disagree | strongly disagree |
|---|---|---|---|---|

Rationale:

_____

_____

_____

4. Most Mexican American families represent the extended family pattern.

| strongly agree | tend to agree | unsure | tend to disagree | strongly disagree |
|---|---|---|---|---|

Rationale:

_____

_____

_____

5. Family roles are very specific and rigid in African American families.

| strongly agree | tend to agree | unsure | tend to disagree | strongly disagree |
|---|---|---|---|---|

Rationale:

_____

_____

_____

6. The Native American concept of family is similar to that of mainstream European Americans.

| strongly agree | tend to agree | unsure | tend to disagree | strongly disagree |
| --- | --- | --- | --- | --- |

Rationale:

_____

_____

_____

7. Mexican American families are patriarchal.

| strongly agree | tend to agree | unsure | tend to disagree | strongly disagree |
| --- | --- | --- | --- | --- |

Rationale:

_____

_____

_____

8. For most Native Americans and Asians, youths are honored and revered.

| strongly agree | tend to agree | unsure | tend to disagree | strongly disagree |
| --- | --- | --- | --- | --- |

Rationale:

_____

_____

_____

## Stereotypes and Generalizations

Because people cannot respond to each and every piece of information to which they are exposed they form categories as an attempt to simplify the world around them. **Stereotypes** refer to categories about people. Categories in general, and stereotypes in particular, are shortcuts in people's thinking. As with most stereotypes applied to individuals, much of the content is inaccurate. We must thus be careful not to form stereotypes about people.

**Generalizations**, on the other hand, can be useful in people's thinking and interacting with others. Generalizations refer to trends over large numbers of individuals (Brislin, 2000). For example, if 100 cases were studied in collectivist and individualistic societies, more collectivists would behave in a manner that emphasized their group's goals, and more individualists would behave in a manner that emphasized their own personal goals. The concept of *trends over large numbers of people* is important to keep in mind whenever culture and cultural differences are discussed. We can use generalizations that are supported by the research literature in our discussions about culture, but should avoid the use of stereotypes.

The following are generalizations that can be made from the content of the *Ethnic Literacy Test*. The responses you will read are generalizations that can be supported in the research literature. One must keep in mind, however, that there will always be cases that do not conform to the generalization and will make discussions more fruitful and engaging. Extend the response to these generalizations by suggesting some implications for education that are related to the specific information presented.

## Communication Differences

1. Newly arrived Mexican American children *may* have difficulty reading words that begin with two consonants. When compared with Standard English, the Spanish language has relatively few consonant clusters.

   **Possible educational implications:**

   _____

   _____

   _____

   _____

2. Non-standard English dialects, like Ebonics, are language systems that operate by rules. While the rules may be different, both standard and non-standard forms of a language operate by rules.

   **Possible educational implications:**

   _____

   _____

   _____

   _____

3. Many Appalachians form the possessive pronoun by adding "n," such as his'n or her'n.

   **Possible educational implications:**

   _____

   _____

   _____

   _____

4. Ebonics, or Black English, is *not* a synonym for Black slang. Ebonics is a dialect of Standard English which, like any language or dialect, has its own slang.

   **Possible educational implications:**

   _____

   _____

   _____

   _____

5. Since the double consonant is not common in the Vietnamese language, Vietnamese children *may* experience problems spelling words that end with a double consonant.

   **Possible educational implications:**

   _____

   _____

   _____

   _____

6. As the Vietnamese language is largely monosyllabic, Vietnamese children may experience difficulty learning to read polysyllabic words.

   **Possible educational implications:**

   _____

   _____

   _____

   _____

7. Native Americans do not all speak the same language — there are more than 400 different languages spoken by the people of the many distinct Nations.

   **Possible educational implications:**

   _____

   _____

   _____

   _____

8. Touching by a teacher and a Mexican American student may result in increased academic achievement as it signals affection and a strong relationship to the child.

   **Possible educational implications:**

   _____

   _____

   _____

   _____

9. Touching the head of a Thai student (and others from some Asian countries) should not be done. The head is considered the most sacred part of the body and may signal the release of the spirit if touched.

   **Possible educational implications:**

   _____

   _____

   _____

   _____

10. African Americans *may* interrupt a speaker with encouraging remarks. Such is the basis for what is commonly referred to as *call and response*, and should not be misjudged as rudeness.

**Possible educational implications:**

_____

_____

_____

_____

## Value Orientations

1. The concept of time for many Native Americans may be quite different from that of European Americans.

**Possible educational implications:**

_____

_____

_____

_____

2. Mexican American religious beliefs include the concept of fatalism, or the belief that God controls much and if something is meant to be, God will make it happen. The individual may, thus, perceive him or herself to have relatively little control over a given situation. In Arabic, the phrase "N'Shalah" (if God wills it) captures this belief.

**Possible educational implications:**

_____

_____

_____

_____

3. Appalachians tend to have strong kinship bonds.

   **Possible educational implications:**

   _____

   _____

   _____

   _____

4. Based on statistics from the Bureau of Labor Statistics, African Americans tend to have a strong work orientation.

   **Possible educational implications:**

   _____

   _____

   _____

   _____

5. Native Americans tend to prefer private rather than public recognition.

   **Possible educational implications:**

   _____

   _____

   _____

   _____

6. Mexican American students generally prefer to work in groups rather than as individuals.

   **Possible educational implications:**

   _____

   _____

   _____

   _____

7. Appalachians have a relatively difficult time adapting to urban life.

   **Possible educational implications:**

   _____

   _____

   _____

   _____

8. African Americans tend to be deeply religious.

   **Possible educational implications:**

   _____

   _____

   _____

   _____

9. For some African Americans (as well as some other groups), to avoid eye contact is a sign of respect.

   **Possible educational implications:**

   _____

   _____

   _____

   _____

10. Among Native Americans, the concept of private ownership is not common.

   **Possible educational implications:**

   _____

   _____

   _____

   _____

## Family Structures and Lifestyles

1. The African American family tends to be equalitarian. That is, mothers and fathers tend to share responsibilities and roles fairly equally.

   **Possible educational implications:**

   _____

   _____

   _____

   _____

2. The majority of Appalachian families follow an extended family pattern.

   **Possible educational implications:**

   _____

   _____

   _____

   _____

3. The Appalachian family tends to be patriarchal with boys being favored.

   **Possible educational implications:**

   _____

   _____

   _____

   _____

4. Most Mexican American families represent the extended family pattern.

   **Possible educational implications:**

   _____

   _____

   _____

   _____

5. Family roles can be rather flexible in African American families.

   **Possible educational implications:**

   _____

   _____

   _____

   _____

6. The Native American concept of family follows the extended pattern.

   **Possible educational implications:**

   _____

   _____

   _____

   _____

7. Mexican American families tend to be patriarchal. That is, the father's decision is usually the final say.

   **Possible educational implications:**

   _____

   _____

   _____

   _____

8. For most Native Americans and Asians, the elderly tend to be honored and revered.

   **Possible educational implications:**

   _____

   _____

   _____

   _____

# Determining Bias in Textbooks

## Purpose

To develop skill in identifying stereotypes and bias in textbooks.

## Instructions

Select a school textbook or other children's book that was printed many years ago. Using the guidelines below, evaluate the book for stereotypes of women, men, various ethnic groups, the elderly, and so forth. Repeat this exercise with a newer textbook and compare your findings.

Title of book: _____ Year of publication: _____

Give a brief description of the book:

_____

_____

_____

1. Analyze the illustrations for stereotypes. What are people doing that may create or perpetuate a stereotype?

    _____

    _____

    _____

    _____

2. Analyze the storyline. What is the role of women or people of color in the story? How are problems presented and resolved?

    _____

    _____

    _____

    _____

3. Look closely at the lifestyles depicted in the book. How are different groups shown?

_____

_____

_____

_____

4. What people seem to have power in the book or story? Who is subservient? How are family relationships and composition represented?

_____

_____

_____

_____

5. From the reader's point of view, are there issues or norms that might limit or restrict one's aspirations or self-esteem?

_____

_____

_____

_____

6. What cultural, social, and economic biases of the author might be evident?

_____

_____

_____

_____

7. Look for certain loaded words that might bias the reader. Are there words with derogatory connotations or overtones?

_____

_____

_____

_____

Now repeat the exercise with a more recent book designed to achieve a similar goal. What differences are evident? To what would you attribute these differences? What cautions or concerns remain from your point of view?

_____

_____

_____

_____

_____

_____

_____

_____

_____

_____

_____

_____

_____

_____

## Activity and Reading 32

# Learning Styles

## Purpose

To analyze learning style differences among students and explore how they impact the classroom.

## Instructions

Read the content below and respond to the questions that follow.

Learning styles are generally considered to be the cognitive processes and instructional settings a student finds most useful and effective while learning. Examples of such cognitive processes on a global scale include coding and decoding, organizing, perceiving, remembering, and reasoning (Hughes and More, 1993). The five most commonly recognized dimensions of learning that are found in the classroom (IBE, 1994) are:

a. **Global — Analytical**. Students who are more global learn best when the overall concepts are presented first, or presented in a meaningful context. Students who are more analytical tend to learn better when information is presented in small pieces and then gradually build up to an overall picture.

b. **Verbal — Imaginal**. Verbal learners tend to learn better from highly verbal explanations or from dictionary-like definitions. These students rely more on words and labels, use verbal regulation of behavior more effectively, and code concepts verbally. The more imaginal learners learn better from images, symbols, and diagrams.

c. **Concrete — Abstract**. Some students learn better when the concept is presented first in its abstract form, perhaps as a rule or principle. Others learn best when the concept is presented in its real form and as it will actually be used. This dimension is sometimes referred to as in-context versus out-of-context teaching and learning.

d. **Reflective — Trial/Error/Feedback**. The reflective learner thinks through the new learning before actually using it. In the Trial/Error/Feedback style, the learner responds more quickly (trial), knowing the answer may not be correct (error), expecting to learn from the teacher's feedback to the response. One learns to ride a bicycle, for instance, using this method.

e. **Modality**. This reflects the fact that some students learn more effectively through seeing, others through hearing, others through touching, and so on.

Each of the above-mentioned learning style preferences can be individual or cultural manifestations. The important thing is that teachers are aware of the differences and that they become skillful at modifying their classrooms to accommodate the various needs or preferences of their students. Consider the next activity.

Listed below are a few differences in people's ways of thinking and interacting.

**Thinking Patterns:** The thinking patterns favored by a culture determine, to a great extent, the way people in that culture learn and teach. Consider some of these contrasting differences.

| Analytic Pattern | Global Pattern |
| --- | --- |
| Operates with facts and data | Operates with ideas |
| Concerned with immediate results | Concerned more with process |
| Highly analytical | Holistic or relational |
| Works well individually | Works well with others |

For students, what might be some of the consequences of the differences listed above?

_____

_____

_____

_____

What are some of the consequences for educators given that they might have a classroom full of students whose learning style preferences may include all of the above?

_____

_____

_____

What modifications in instruction might facilitate learning for students in each category? Your response should consider such aspects as pacing, experiential versus didactic presentations, as well as assessment and motivational strategies.

**Global—Analytical**

_____

_____

_____

**Verbal—Imaginal**

_____

_____

_____

**Concrete—Abstract**

_____

_____

_____

**Reflective—Trial/Error/Feedback**

_____

_____

_____

**Modality**

_____

_____

_____

# The Goals of an Education
# That Reflects Diversity

## Purpose

To understand the broad goals of diversity and examine them in terms of existing curricula.

## Instructions

Read and discuss the following *Goals of an Education That Reflects Diversity.*

Over the years, numerous theoreticians and practitioners have proposed various definitions and goals for multicultural education. As expected, these statements have evolved as the field itself has broadened and redefined itself. The following list attempts to integrate many of the various goals of multicultural education. The approach and some of the subsequent activities are modifications of a model developed by Davidman and Davidman (1994).

**Goal 1**: Improve understanding of the concept of pluralism in American society. Pluralism in this context must consider such sources of cultural identity as nationality, ethnicity, race, gender, socioeconomic status, religion, sexual orientation, health, and ability/disability (the attributes of culture identified earlier). One must look particularly at how each of these has impacted the individual as well as the group.

**Goal 2**: Expand the knowledge base of culture and the many different groups found in the United States (or any country) as well as abroad. At a content level, this considers curriculum inclusion of previously marginalized groups (e.g., women, people of color) as well as expansion to address multiple perspectives (e.g., racism in practice). At a process level, this considers pedagogical and communication processes.

**Goal 3**: Improve intergroup as well as intragroup interactions. This demands attention to such issues as cross-cultural understanding and interaction, attribution as well as assessment across groups, and conflict management. Teachers thus must broaden their instructional repertoire so that it reflects an understanding of the various groups they will teach. Students must learn to communicate effectively across groups as well as develop the skills of collaboration that are needed for group problem-solving whether within or between groups.

**Goal 4**: Empower action-oriented, reflective decisionmakers who are able and willing to be socially and politically active in the school, community, nation, and world. This goal is not only concerned with developing the knowledge and skill of practicing teachers but is also concerned with transferring this knowledge and skill to the pupils in their charge. Thus, individuals become proactive teachers and reflective practitioners who can ultimately prepare reflective citizen-actors, both of whom are able and willing to work for change in an interdependent world.

### Discussion Questions

What do you interpret *each* of these goals to mean? Either in writing or in small groups, discuss the meaning of each of these goals.

**Goal 1**

_____

_____

_____

_____

_____

_____

**Goal 2**

_____

_____

_____

_____

_____

_____

**Goal 3**

_____

_____

_____

_____

_____

**Goal 4**

_____

_____

_____

_____

How do you think _each_ of these goals might be addressed in a variety of content areas (i.e., math, science, social studies, etc.)? Be as creative as you can as you consider how these goals might be put into action.

**Goal 1**

_____

_____

_____

_____

_____

**Goal 2**

_____

_____

_____

_____

_____

_____

## Goal 3

_____

_____

_____

_____

_____

_____

## Goal 4

_____

_____

_____

_____

_____

_____

# Modifying Existing Instructional Material to Reflect the Goals of Diversity

## Purpose

To apply the four Goals of Diversity to a range of educational material, including existing lesson or unit plans.

## Instructions

The goals stated in the previous activity can be easily put into practice in most content areas. One can, for instance, review a particular lesson or unit plan, paying particular attention to how each of the goals can be addressed. Each of the goals can be turned into a question that teachers are able to address in a given lesson or unit. Use the following as a guide. Then you will be provided with a few examples of how lessons that utilize this approach might be developed. Finally, you will be asked to modify a lesson of your own.

1. How can the content and strategies of this particular lesson or unit improve student understanding of the concept of pluralism in American society while improving educational equity?

2. How can the content and strategies of this particular lesson or unit expand the knowledge base of culture and the many different groups found in the United States as well as abroad? Is the content accurate, inclusive, and free of bias? Does it give the whole picture? Does it strive to reduce or correct racist impressions?

3. How can the content and strategies of this particular lesson or unit improve intergroup and intragroup interactions? Are assessment strategies broad and inclusive? How is collaboration built into the activity? How can group harmony be improved?

4. How can the content and strategies of this particular lesson or unit empower action-oriented, reflective decisionmakers who are able and willing to be socially and politically active in the school, community, nation, and world?

Following are three examples of lesson or unit plans that have been modified to consider the above goals.

## Lesson One
## The Sense of Taste: Addressing the Goals of Diversity

*(developed by C. Jeffrey Dykhuizen)*

The following is an example of how a typical science lesson on the sense of taste can be modified to address the goals of diversity.

......................................................................................................................................

### Favorite Flavors and the Individual

Following the completion of a rather typical lesson that asks students to "map" the tongue and identify where the taste buds for sweet, salty, bitter, and sour are located, engage students in a discussion of their favorite foods. To facilitate processing of the lesson, ask students where on their tongue they would be most likely to taste the flavor of their favorite food (i.e., ice cream would most likely be tasted on the tip of the tongue).

Find out by a show of hands how many have a favorite food that is sweet; sour; bitter; salty. What taste do most students prefer? Have students hypothesize why they think this might be.

Ask students if they have ever eaten a very delicious, bitter food. A stupendous sour food. A scrumptious salty food. Where? When? What?

Are students' favorite foods completely and exclusively one of the four major flavors, or a combination of flavors? What is their strongest preference? Their favorite combination? Are there other flavors that students identify other than the four given in the lesson? Is spicy a flavor?

### Multicultural Taste Extension

Discuss the foods of different countries and cultures. Do certain cultures seem to emphasize different flavors in their cooking? Have students discuss why they think certain groups of people prefer certain flavors.

Extend the lesson by asking how many of the students like pickles. How do pickles taste? Are they sweet or sour? Can they be both? What are the various combinations of tastes that go into the flavor of a pickle? Where would you taste this on your tongue?

**Goal 1:** Explain the nature and evolution of pickles as a means to preserve foods. Nearly all cultures make pickles of some form or another. Discuss the various types of pickles students can find in their local food store. Can foods other than cucumbers be pickled? Other vegetables? Grains? Meats? What pickled foods did various immigrant groups bring with them to the Americas? What pickled foods were common to the indigenous groups in the Americas?

**Goal 2:** Compare the tastes of varieties of pickles. It may be best to initially compare the tastes of various pickles purchased at the local store (i.e., sweet cucumber pickles, dill pickles, mixed hot pickles, etc.).

Next, bring out pickles from different cultures. Japanese pickled plum or radish, Korean kimchi, and German sauerkraut should provide good contrast. Explore reasons why a particular type of pickle is common to a particular culture. Discuss the geography of the country/culture in which that pickle is found. Which types of pickles do students prefer? Dislike? Why? Which type of pickle was most like ones they had eaten?

**Goal 3:** In small groups, have students analyze a variety of pickles. Which pickles are mostly sweet? Sour? Have students bring in samples of pickled foods found in their home and community. Have students explain why their own family prefers certain pickled foods. Have students discuss why they think humans have a sense of taste. What survival purposes must this have served? Do all humans have the same sense of taste? Why do they think certain cultures prefer certain tastes?

**Goal 4:** Have students analyze the impact on health of pickles. Do all people consider them a healthy food? For instance, some consider pickled foods to be too high in sodium content. What considerations must be made when eating pickled foods? What changes have been evident in various societies with regard to foods that are high in sodium?

Are there certain pickled foods that you would like to see served in your school cafeteria? Available in area stores? How might you go about making your wishes known?

## Lesson Two
## Human Diversity and the Human Figure

*(developed by Jacqueline M. Szemplak)*

The following is a lesson extension of a sculptural art project studying the human figure from a diverse perspective. The lesson can be used with middle and secondary level students.

The following extension has been modified from an art lesson dealing with the human figure. Instead of studying the human figure solely from a Western perspective, students will see examples of sculptures from other areas of the world. As an introduction to the lesson, students will write down their personal thoughts and beliefs on what they consider to be beautiful in a sculpture. What attributes would it have? What type of dress might it have, if any? What would its proportions be? What would be the overall mood of the piece? Would it look like anyone they know, or any famous piece of artwork? Students might generate their own list.

As a multicultural extension, students would view examples of figural sculptures from different time periods and different cultures around the world. Some examples might include Mayan, Egyptian, West African, Japanese, ancient India, and any of the many multicultural modern American sculptures. Then, in small groups and using the list they made earlier, students will discuss which of these sculptures best fits their description of beauty. Will they need to change or modify their original ideas? What do they believe was the intent of each artist? What are the various reactions of viewers of each piece? What elements reflective of the culture are evident in the piece? What materials were used to create the piece? Then, as an entire class, students should construct their universal list of characteristics they believe should be evident in a piece of sculpture. Eventually, they will use their own criteria as a guideline to make and evaluate their own sculptures.

**Goal 1:** Students will analyze how their own culture views the human figure and discuss why and how they were ingrained with a Western view of art. They can discuss how art serves as a form of identity for a culture, subculture, or ethnic group. Forms of art examined may be political, gender-related, religious, or another form that reflects a particular time period or social context. Students should discuss the social and political impacts that Western art forms have had on them.

**Goal 2:** The teacher should guide the students to define the human figure and beauty from a multicultural perspective. This can be accomplished by viewing a variety of sculptures from around the world. Students should come to realize that beauty is culturally defined and that it varies from culture to culture. While not all of the sculptures viewed will be considered beautiful by the criteria of Western art, students should understand that each are considered beautiful and may hold deep cultural meanings in the cultures in which they were created.

**Goal 3:** Students will improve intergroup relations by working cooperatively in groups. They will discuss their own views of figural sculptures as well as the views of others in their class. They will collectively refine the ideas of sculptural beauty from a multicultural perspective. They will then work in small groups to create a sculpture that reflects the criteria they have decided upon.

**Goal 4:** When the small groups have completed their sculpture, they will share them with the entire class. What considerations should be made while viewing each sculpture? Would all people define this as good artwork? Why? Is it museum quality, or might it be considered folk art? Why? What is its best quality? What changes would you want to see if you were a museum curator? How would you make your wishes known? How might you encourage others to view figural sculpture from other ethnic or cultural groups?

## Lesson Three
## Diversity in the Animal Kingdom

*(developed by Kim Elliott)*

The following multicultural lesson extension suitable for the early years illustrates how a science lesson might be used to introduce the concept of diversity. While this lesson specifically targets bears as the animal of focus, it can easily be modified for other animal species. The following extension has been prepared with kindergarten children in mind.

........................................................................................................................................................

Most kindergarten teachers in my district do a brief unit on bears, without addressing the "real" aspect of the animals. Teachers tend to use bear stories and stuffed animals to approach the unit, and integrate a variety of arts-and-craft-type activities to engage children. This may be fine to introduce the lesson and perhaps to personalize it, but time on this aspect could and should be kept to a minimum. Children might be asked if they have a favorite bear as a lead-in to the lesson, but they should then concentrate on the more "real" aspects of the animal, as well as on the diversity of bears and how it might relate to humans. Here is one way in which this might be accomplished.

**Goal 1:** Read a story about bears and ask children where they might be able to see a bear. Ask if all bears at the zoo look the same. Why don't they all look alike? Ask children if they think all bears come from the same place? Discuss with children that even though there may be many different kinds of bears, they are each unique and special in their own way. Show pictures of different types of bear, and have children point out the obvious similarities and differences (e.g., size, shape, color, etc.).

**Goal 2:** Use books and various photos to show children that bears do not all come from the same place. It is here that a teacher might begin to introduce a globe or map while discussing different environments in which bears are found. Have children attempt to match pictures of different bears to a variety of environments and suggest why they think a certain bear might be found in a particular region. You may use a variety of bears and locations, such as the panda from China, the polar bear from the arctic, and grizzly bears from mountainous regions. Note that the koala from Australia is *not* a bear. This might be introduced early in the unit, and children can explore why people tend to classify it as such. This might be used as an example of stereotyping at a later time.

**Goal 3:** Have the children work in groups to draw the environments from which several bears have originated. Have them share their pictures as a group with the rest of the class. Discuss with the children the different types of foods that each bear eats. Explain that the reason the bears eat these different types of foods is that they are naturally occurring in the environments in which they live (e.g., panda-bamboo, polar bear-fish, grizzly-fish). Bring in samples of bamboo and fish for the children to examine. Which of these foods would they eat? Why? Why not? Have them consider if people in these parts of the world eat similar foods. Why? Why not? Discuss that just as bears' eating habits differ from region to region, so, too, do the eating habits of people who live in different regions.

**Goal 4:** Bring together all the different ideas children have been discussing. Discuss with children that just as there are different types of bears in the world, there are also different types of people. Also discuss that like the bears, people from different parts of the world live in different environments, eat different foods, and enjoy different types of activities. Using the bears as parallels to humans, go back to the original idea of the unit to explore that we are all humans, and are all unique and special, even if we come from different parts of the world.

As an extension, let the children plan an imaginary trip to one of the regions to see their favorite bear in its natural environment. During the trip, you might study such things as the region's geography, climate, native peoples, and foods.

# Now It's Your Turn: Modify a Lesson to Address the Goals of Diversity

## Purpose

To apply the *Goals of Diversity* to a lesson you develop.

## Instructions

Select an already prepared lesson plan for the subject area you plan to teach. Or develop your own lesson or unit plan. Review this lesson with the four goals in mind, and respond to the questions as stated below.

1. How can the content and strategies of this particular lesson or unit improve student understanding of the concept of pluralism in American society while improving educational equity?

   _____

   _____

   _____

   _____

   _____

   _____

2. How can the content and strategies of this particular lesson or unit expand the knowledge base of culture and the many different groups found in the United States as well as abroad? Is the content accurate, inclusive, and free of bias? Does it give the whole picture? Does it strive to reduce or correct racist impressions?

   _____

   _____

   _____

   _____

3. How can the content and strategies of this particular lesson or unit improve inter-group and intragroup interactions? Are assessment strategies broad and inclusive? How is collaboration built into the activity? How can group harmony be improved?

_____

_____

_____

_____

_____

_____

4. How can the content and strategies of this particular lesson or unit empower action-oriented, reflective decisionmakers who are able and willing to be socially and politically active in the school, community, nation, and world?

_____

_____

_____

_____

_____

_____

# Inventory of Cross-Cultural Sensitivity (ICCS)

## Purpose

To complete a self-assessment instrument with regard to your intercultural experiences.

## Instructions

The following questionnaire asks you to rate your agreement or disagreement with a series of statements. Please respond honestly as there are no correct answers. You will find another copy of this in the last section of the workbook that you can complete toward the end of the course. You can compare your responses from the beginning to the end of the book.

Please circle the number that best corresponds to your level of agreement with each statement below:

| | *1 = Strongly Disagree    7 = Strongly Agree* |
|---|---|
| 1. I speak only one language | 1...2...3...4...5...6...7 |
| 2. The way other people express themselves is very interesting to me | 1...2...3...4...5...6...7 |
| 3. I enjoy being with people from other cultures | 1...2...3...4...5...6...7 |
| 4. Foreign influence in our country threatens our national identity | 1...2...3...4...5...6...7 |
| 5. Others' feelings rarely influence decisions I make | 1...2...3...4...5...6...7 |
| 6. I cannot eat with chopsticks | 1...2...3...4...5...6...7 |
| 7. I avoid people who are different from me | 1...2...3...4...5...6...7 |
| 8. It is better that people from other cultures avoid one another | 1...2...3...4...5...6...7 |
| 9. Culturally mixed marriages are wrong | 1...2...3...4...5...6...7 |
| 10. I think people are basically alike | 1...2...3...4...5...6...7 |
| 11. I have never lived outside my own culture for any great length of time | 1...2...3...4...5...6...7 |

| | *1 = Strongly Disagree    7 = Strongly Agree* |
|---|---|
| 12. I have foreigners to my home on a regular basis | 1...2...3...4...5...6...7 |
| 13. It makes me nervous to talk to people who are different from me | 1...2...3...4...5...6...7 |
| 14. I enjoy studying about people from other cultures | 1...2...3...4...5...6...7 |
| 15. People from other cultures do things differently because they do not know any other way | 1...2...3...4...5...6...7 |
| 16. There is usually more than one good way to get things done | 1...2...3...4...5...6...7 |
| 17. I listen to music from another culture on a regular basis | 1...2...3...4...5...6...7 |
| 18. I decorate my home or room with artifacts from other countries | 1...2...3...4...5...6...7 |
| 19. I feel uncomfortable when in a crowd of people | 1...2...3...4...5...6...7 |
| 20. The very existence of humanity depends upon our knowledge about other people | 1...2...3...4...5...6...7 |
| 21. Residential neighborhoods should be culturally separated | 1...2...3...4...5...6...7 |
| 22. I have many friends | 1...2...3...4...5...6...7 |
| 23. I dislike eating foods from other cultures | 1...2...3...4...5...6...7 |
| 24. I think about living within another culture in the future | 1...2...3...4...5...6...7 |
| 25. Moving into another culture would be easy | 1...2...3...4...5...6...7 |
| 26. I like to discuss issues with people from other cultures | 1...2...3...4...5...6...7 |
| 27. There should be tighter controls on the number of immigrants allowed into my country | 1...2...3...4...5...6...7 |
| 28. The more I know about people, the more I dislike them | 1...2...3...4...5...6...7 |
| 29. I read more national news than international news in the daily newspaper | 1...2...3...4...5...6...7 |
| 30. Crowds of foreigners frighten me | 1...2...3...4...5...6...7 |
| 31. When something newsworthy happens I seek out someone from that part of the world to discuss the issue with | 1...2...3...4...5...6...7 |
| 32. I eat ethnic foods at least twice a week | 1...2...3...4...5...6...7 |

## Scoring the ICCS

The ICCS can be scored by subscales. Simply insert the numbered circled on the test form in the spaces provided under each subscale heading. Reverse the values for the items marked with an asterisk (*) . For instance, reverse scoring results in:

$$7=1, 6=2, 5=3, 4=4, 3=5, 2=6, 1=7$$

Then add the values in each column for the subscale score. A total ICCS score is obtained by adding the various subscale scores together. Individuals can be ranked relative to others in a particular group. You can also identify relative strengths and weaknesses that may lead to more focused orientation and planning.

ICCS Scoring Guide    Subject ID_____

| C Scale | | B Scale | | I Scale | |
|---------|---|---------|---|---------|---|
| item | score | item | score | item | score |
| 1* | ____ | 2 | ____ | 3 | ____ |
| 6* | ____ | 7* | ____ | 8* | ____ |
| 11* | ____ | 13* | ____ | 14 | ____ |
| 12 | ____ | 19* | ____ | 20 | ____ |
| 17 | ____ | 25* | ____ | 26 | ____ |
| 18 | ____ | 30 | ____ | 31 | ____ |
| 23* | ____ | | | | |
| 24 | ____ | | | | |
| 29* | ____ | | | | |
| 32 | ____ | | | | |

| A Scale | | E Scale |
| --- | --- | --- |
| item | score | item |
| 4* | ____ | 5* |
| 9* | ____ | 10 |
| 15* | ____ | 16 |
| 21* | ____ | 22 |
| 27* | ____ | 28* |

### Totals

C Scale = ____

B Scale = ____

I Scale = ____

A Scale = ____

E Scale = ____


Total ICCS Score  =  ____

* Reverse-score all items marked with an asterisk because these are negatively worded items.

## Interpreting the Inventory of Cross-Cultural Sensitivity

The ICCS is a 32-item instrument that provides dimensional scores for individuals on each of five subscales. Individuals can be ranked relative to others from high to low levels of sensitivity on issues and experiences related to cross-cultural or intercultural interaction (the higher the score, the more sensitive an individual is presumed to be). While the ICCS should not be used in a predictive manner, results can be used to raise people's awareness of some of the issues to consider prior to intercultural interaction.

The five subscales and the range of scores include:

| *Subscale* | *Range of Scores* |
|---|---|
| Cultural Integration (C Scale): assesses the degree to which an individual integrates elements from cultures other than their own into their daily activities. | 10–70 |
| Behavioral Scale (B Scale): assesses the degree to which an individual has adopted behavior that is new or has a degree of comfort when interacting with others. | 6–42 |
| Intellectual Interaction (I Scale): assesses the degree to which an individual seeks out knowledge of other cultural orientations. | 6–42 |
| Attitude Toward Others (A Scale): assesses the degree of openness toward others. | 5–35 |
| Empathy Scale (E Scale): assesses the degree to which an individual identifies with the feelings of others. | 5–35 |
| Total Score Range | 32–224 |

Now compare your results on each subscale with those when you first completed the inventory at the beginning of the book (see Activity 2).

What surprised you most when comparing your scores?

_____

_____

_____

_____

In what areas have you shown the most growth? The least? To what would you attribute these changes (or lack of changes)?

_____

_____

_____

_____

_____

_____

_____

_____

What questions or issues did this instrument fail to address that you believe would better demonstrate how you have grown or changed?

_____

_____

_____

_____

_____

_____

_____

_____

## The Technical Details of the ICCS (or the fine print)

Content validity looks to the extent to which a test encompasses a reasonable sample of the responses or behaviors that characterize the variable of interest. Thirty-two statements that effectively differentiated individuals varying in amount of intercultural experience, and which when factor analyzed using varimax rotation loaded highly on one dimension and maintained eignevalues greater than 1.0, were retained in this version of the ICCS.

Construct validity refers to the degree to which the instrument succeeds in measuring what it purports to measure. The ICCS has effectively differentiated individuals having extensive intercultural experience (two or more years living and/or working overseas) from those having little or no intercultural experience (undergraduate university students living in northeastern Ohio). Those having limited intercultural experience have ranked between these two groups. The ICCS has demonstrated the ability to differentiate individuals having received cross-cultural training from control group members (Broaddus, 1986; Cushner, 1989).

Reliability refers to the extent that the instrument obtains consistent and stable results. Reliability estimates for the ICCS appear to be quite stable:

C Scale = .9415; B Scale = .7009; I Scale = .8869; A Scale = .7860; E Scale = .5239.

# Glossary

**Ambiguous:** Unclear. In the cross-cultural context this refers to the lack of clarity that typifies many interactions that still requires an individual to respond.

**Anxiety:** An emotional state of general and undefined nervousness that often exists in an intercultural encounter due to the unfamiliarity of another's behavior.

**Attribution:** The judgments people make about others based on the behavior they observe.

**Belonging:** The need people have to feel as if they have a role and purpose in a given setting or context.

**Categorization:** The process of dividing stimuli into classes or groups according to a particular system. In the cultural context, this refers to the manner by which a culture teaches its members to view the world around them.

**Collective group:** Refers to members of a group that tend to identify with one another who will often be deferred to when making decisions.

**Communication Differences:** Generally refers to group-level differences in both verbal as well as non-verbal modes.

**Differentiation:** Refers to the process of distinguishing the finer points between elements of a given category, as a wine connoisseur is able to do. In the cross-cultural context, this refers to distinctions made between aspects of a category that are important to a given group of people.

**Disability:** Refers to the inability to do something that is desirable.

**Disconfirmed expectations:** Refers to the tendency individuals may have that causes them to become upset or uncomfortable, not because of the specific circumstances they encounter, but because the situation differs from what they expect.

**Ethnicity:** Ethnicity refers to the knowledge, beliefs and behavior patterns shared by a group of people with the same history and the same language.

**Ethnocentrism:** The tendency people have to evaluate others from their own cultural reference.

**Faulty attributions:** Inaccurate judgments made about others. In the cross-cultural context this refers to judgments made by an observer using criteria that are not used by the particular actor in a given situation.

**Fundamental attribution error:** The tendency people have to judge others using different criteria than they would use to judge themselves.

**Gender:** Socially defined category in which the biological specialization of male and female are transformed by associating specific personality, role, and status traits to each sex.

**Generalization:** Refers to the tendency of a majority of people in a cultural group to hold certain values and beliefs, and to engage in certain patterns of behavior. Thus, this information can be supported by research and can be applied to a large percentage of a population or group.

**Group allegiances:** Tendency to identify and make major decisions according to those preferred by a group to which one identifies, which can be ethnic, religious, national, etc.

**Health:** Health is culturally defined according to a particular group's view of what physical, mental, and emotional states constitute a "healthy" person. The "expert" opinion of the medical profession usually guides a view of health in the industrialized world, although alternative systems such as acupuncture, holistic medicine, and faith healing are available; the acceptance of which varies widely both within and between social groups.

**Individual interests:** Tendency to identify and make major decisions according to one's own individual preferences as opposed to those of the group.

**Ingroups:** Refers to those individuals one feels psychologically closest to and who often share rather intimate knowledge and interpersonal relationships.

**Language:** A collection of meaningful sounds used to communicate messages to others.

**Learning style:** A consistent pattern of behavior and performance by which an individual approaches educational experiences; learning style is derived from cultural socialization and individual personality, as well as from the broader influence of human development.

**Model minority:** Refers to those groups who excel in school and who appear to have overcome discrimination.

**Nationality:** Identification and the state of belonging to a particular nation-state.

**Nonverbal communication:** Means of communication that are unspoken and may or may not accompany verbal communication. Refers to such things as gestures, facial expressions, use of space, etc.

**Objective culture:** The visible, tangible aspects of a group of people, including such things as the artifacts produced, the clothing worn and food that is eaten.

**Outgroups:** Refers to those persons generally kept at a psychological distance from oneself.

**Prejudice:** Non-reflective judgments about others that are harsh, discriminatory, or involve rejection.

**Privilege:** A special advantage or right granted or enjoyed by certain individuals or groups.

**Race:** Biologically speaking, it refers to the clustering of inherited physical characteristics that favor adaptation to a particular ecological area. Race is culturally defined in the sense that different societies emphasize different sets of physical characteristics when referring to the concept of race. Thus, race is an important social characteristic, not because of its biology, but because of its cultural meaning in any given social group or society.

**Religion:** Religion is defined on the basis of a shared set of ideas about the relationship of the earth and the people on it to a deity or deities and a shared set of rules for living moral values that will enhance that relationship.

**Rituals:** A series of acts performed in a prescribed manner, usually in conjunction with a religious or spiritual ceremony.

**Role-based behavior:** Patterns of behavior expected to be carried out in a manner deemed appropriate for a given position one may hold.

**Sexuality:** Particular patterns of sexual self-identification, behavior, and interpersonal relationships that identify one as either male or female.

**Situational behavior:** Behavior of an individual or a group that is characteristic in a particular setting or context.

**Social status:** Refers to the degree to which an individual has power, influence, or leadership in his or her social group.

**Socialization:** The process whereby individuals learn what is appropriate to be a functioning member of a particular group, such as family, work, or social group.

**Spirituality:** Spirituality generally refers to a set of ideas about the relationship of an individual to the earth and to deities. Whereas religion is generally group-oriented and formal in its organzation, spirituality can refer to a more personal experience.

**Stereotypes:** Beliefs about the personal attributes of a group based on the inaccurate generalizations used to describe all members of the group, thus ignoring individual differences.

**Subjective culture:** Refers to the invisible, intangible aspects of a group, including such things as attitudes, values, norms of behavior; the things typically kept in people's minds.

**Superstitions:** Belief or practices resulting from ignorance or false conception of causality.

**Values:** Internalized beliefs that provide social cohesion among group members that are often codified into laws or rules for living, such as the Ten Commandments for Christians and Jews or the Hippocratic Oath for doctors.

# References

Akron Beacon Journal (2000). *Ah, but the mystery.* p. A12.

Bellah, R.; Madsen, R.; Sullivan, W.; Swindler, A.; and Tipton, S. *Habits of the Heart: Individualism and Commitment in American Life.* (New York: Harper and Row, 1985).

Berger, P. L. and Berger, B. *Sociology: A Biographical Approach.* (New York: Basic Books, 1972).

Brislin, R. *Understanding Culture's Influence on Behavior, 2nd ed.* (Fort Worth, TX: Harcourt Brace Jovanovich, 2000).

Chomsky, N. *Cartesian Linguistics.* (New York: Harper and Row, 1966).

Cushner, K. and Brislin, R. *Intercultural Interactions: A Practical Guide, 2nd ed.* (Thousand Oaks, CA: SAGE Publications, 1996).

Cushner, K.; McClelland, A.and Safford, P. *Human Diversity in Education: An Integrative Approach, 5th ed.* (New York: McGraw-Hill, 2006).

Davidman L. and Davidman P. T. *Teaching with a Multicultural Perspective: A Practical Guide.* (New York: Longman, 1994).

Drum, J.; Hughes, S.; and Otero, G. *Global Winners: 74 Learning Activities for Inside and Outside the Classroom.* (Yarmouth, ME: Intercultural Press, 1994).

Gilligan, C. *In a Different Voice.* (Cambridge, MA: Harvard University Press, 1983).

Gollnick, D. and Chinn, P. C. *Multicultural Education in a Pluralistic Society, 3rd ed.* (New York: Macmillan, 1990).

Herek, G. M. "On Heterosexual Masculinity: Some Psychical Consequences of the Social Construction of Gender and Sexuality." *American Behavioral Scientist*, 1986, *29*(5), p. 5.

Hughes, P. and More, A. J. *Learning Styles/Patterns and Aboriginal Students.* Presentation to the World Conference on Indigenous People's Education. (Wollongong, Australia, December 1993).

International Bureau of Education. *Educational Innovation and Information.* (Geneva, Switzerland, September 1994).

LeVay, S. and Hunter, D.H. "Evidence for a Biological Influence in Male Homosexuality." *Scientific American,* 1994, 270, pp. 44-49.

McIntosh, P. *White Privilege and Male Privilege: A Personal Account of Coming to See Correspondences though Work in Women's Studies.* Working Paper No. 189. (Wellesley, MA: Wellesley College Center for Research on Women, 1988).

Pedersen, P. *A Handbook for Developing Multicultural Awareness, 3rd ed.* (Alexandria, VA: American Association for Counseling and Development, 2000).

Ponterotto, J. and Pedersen, P. *Preventing Prejudice: A Guide for Counselors and Educators.* (Newbury Park, CA: SAGE Publications, 1993).

Summerfield, E. *Survival Kit for Multicultural Living.* (Yarmouth, ME: Intercultural Press, 1997).

Vonnegut, K. Afterword, in F. Klagsburn (Ed.) *Free to Be...You and Me.* (New York: McGraw-Hill, 1974).